SELECTIONS FROM

The Art of Party-Crashing
in Medieval Iraq

Bunan

SELECTIONS FROM

The Art of
Party-
Crashing
in Medieval Iraq

al-Khaṭīb al-Baghdādī

TRANSLATED AND ILLUSTRATED BY
Emily Selove

Syracuse University Press

Copyright © 2012 by Syracuse University Press
Syracuse, New York 13244-5290

All Rights Reserved

First Edition 2012

15   16   17   18   19   6   5   4   3   2

Translated from *Al-tatfil wa hikayat al-tufayliyin wa akhbaruhum wa nawadir
kalamihim wa ash'aruhum.* The Chester Beatty Library gives permission
for the text of CBL Ar 3851, as translated by Emily Selove and published
in this volume. The Trustees of the Chester Beatty Library, Dublin, are
the rights holders of the original text.

∞ The paper used in this publication meets the minimum requirements
of the American National Standard for Information Sciences—Permanence
of Paper for Printed Library Materials, ANSI Z39.48-1992.

For a listing of books published and distributed by Syracuse University Press,
visit www.SyracuseUniversityPress.syr.edu.

ISBN: 978-0-8156-3298-6 (cloth)   978-0-8156-5179-6

Library of Congress Cataloging-in-Publication Data
Khatib al-Baghdadi, Abu Bakr Ahmad ibn 'Ali, 1002–1071.
[Tatfil wa-hikayat al-tufayliyin wa-akhbarihim wa-nawadir kalamihim
wa-ash'arihim. Selections. English]
Selections from the art of party-crashing in medieval Iraq / al-Khatib
al-Baghdadi ; translated and illustrated by Emily Selove.
p. cm.
Includes bibliographical references.
ISBN 978-0-8156-3298-6 (cloth : alk. paper) 1. Parasitism (Social sciences)
in literature. 2. Arabic poetry—750–1258—History and criticism.
3. Parasitism (Social sciences)—Anecdotes. 4. Anecdotes—Arab
countries. I. Selove, Emily. II. Title.
PJ7519.P32K48213 2012
892.7'83407—dc23   2012038545

Manufactured in the United States of America

Contents

Contents

Illustrations

Translator's Note

The Book of Party-Crashing was compiled in the eleventh century by al-Khatib al-Baghdadi (d. 1071), a Muslim preacher and scholar of the hadith (reports on the deeds and sayings of the prophet Muhammad).[1] Al-Khatib is known mainly for his work *Tarikh Baghdad* (The History of Baghdad), which describes thousands of Baghdadi scholars. Like most of his writing, his *History* was intended as an aid for students of the hadith.

In its lighthearted subject matter, al-Khatib's *Book of Party-Crashing* represents a departure from his more serious-minded religious scholarship. Nevertheless, even this work begins with hadith demonstrating the Prophet's generosity and lenient attitude

---

1. Al-Khatib al-Baghdadi, *Al-tatfil wa hikayat al-tufayliyin wa akhbaruhum wa nawadir kalamihim wa ash'aruhum.*

toward the uninvited guest. Al-Khatib provides multiple versions of each hadith, with careful attention to their sources, so that even in this seemingly frivolous project (as he himself characterizes it in his introduction), his scholarly colors shine through. Nevertheless, the party-crashers in this text engage in some lighthearted blasphemy and plenty of drinking (all relatively mild, however, in comparison to many contemporaneous Arabic texts on the same subject).

This book represents one of thousands of untranslated works of medieval Arabic literature,[2] whose many delights and surprises are consequently unknown to much of the English-speaking world. In many ways it is a typical example of monographic

---

2. In calling this time period "medieval," I am applying Western terminology where it does not necessarily belong. For a full condemnation of those who use Western terminology in this fashion, see Thomas Bauer's review "In Search of 'Post-classical Literature.'" I persist in my error, however, in order to promote awareness of the fact that medieval European literature evolved in tandem with, even partly as a result of, contemporaneous Arabic literature, the authors of which, in turn, drew no less from classical texts for inspiration than did their European fellows. No line need be drawn down the center of the Mediterranean when discussing certain elements of literature produced during this time period, which is known to English speakers as "medieval."

adab (Arabic belles lettres), including both instruc-
tive and entertaining elements side by side in a pleas-
ing bouquet. I hope this translation is the first of
many works of medieval Arabic humor that I present
to the English-speaking reader. I have already begun
translation of another eleventh-century Arabic text
about party-crashing, *The Imitation of Abu al-Qasim*,
as indeed party-crashers were a favorite topic of the
time. For a fun and informative introduction to this
work and to other similar Arabic texts, I recommend
Geert Jan van Gelder's *Of Dishes and Discourse: Classical Arabic Literary Representations of Food* (also published under the title *God's Banquet*).

I have based my translation of al-Khatib's work
on the manuscript held in the Chester Beatty Library
of Dublin, Arabic manuscript 3851. The chapter
titles are (occasionally loose) translations of the
original chapter titles presented in this manuscript,
except for the chapters "Early Party-Crashing,"
"Mention of the Party-Crashers' Conversations,
Advice, and Poetry," and "Accounts of Bunan, the
Party-Crasher," all conglomerations of several adja-
cent chapters.

Some anecdotes presented in the manuscript
were not translated in this volume. Most of these
anecdotes (twenty-five total) are repetitions of previous anecdotes, with different citations. These were
provided meticulously by al-Khatib, whose scholarly

instincts led him to include as full a collection of sources as possible. Several untranslated anecdotes are simply elaborations on the chain of transmission. The other missing anecdotes are mostly poetry (fifteen), because poetry is quite frankly difficult to translate (and some say impossible), especially if one renders, as I have, each translation into rhymed verse. I did so in hopes of providing as enjoyable and authentic experience of the Arabic originals as possible, which themselves employ a monorhyme scheme.

I have chosen to include the chains of transmission at the beginning of each anecdote because they were clearly important to al-Khatib, whose work as a hadith scholar demanded careful scrutiny of these chains in order to verify each account's veracity. Sometimes these chains of transmission enter into the anecdote itself, though for the most part, they can safely be skipped by readers of this translation. If the reader is curious about a name mentioned, many of them can be found in the *Encyclopaedia of Islam* or volume 311 of the *Dictionary of Literary Biography*.

Acknowledgments

I began this translation as an undergraduate at Cornell University, where it served as my senior thesis in 2006, and continued working on it off and on throughout graduate school at UCLA. This work has been so long in the making that I must have forgotten some people who helped make it possible. I should first thank them, whoever they may be. Next I should thank Devin Stewart, who first suggested the text as suitable to my interests and abilities. He thereby launched what I hope will prove a lifelong love affair with medieval Arabic party-crashing. I should also thank Cornell University's College Scholar Program, which allowed me to invent my own major ("Literary Translation of Medieval Arabic Prosimetrum"), thus providing me the flexibility to begin this translation as an undergraduate.

Shawkat Toorawa, my thesis adviser at Cornell, not only spent countless extra hours guiding me on my first steps into the ocean of Arabic literature, providing detailed commentary and advice on many of these translated anecdotes, but also warmed my heart with his friendship and humor. My other undergraduate committee members, Kenneth McClane (professor of English), Stan Taft (professor of art), and Ross Brann (professor of Arabic literature), were all similarly inspiring and helpful. Indeed, Ross Brann's Qur'anic Arabic class first excited my interest in the language. Munther Younes was also always willing to advise me and encourage my interests in Arabic. I must also thank Michael Cooperson, who spent many hours reviewing these translations and generally excelling at his job as my graduate adviser at UCLA. He is an inspiration to me as a brilliant scholar, translator, and illustrator. I also thank Bassam 'Abd al-Wahhab al-Jabi, most recent editor of the manuscript used in this translation, and Antonella Ghersetti, Italian translator of this text, both of whose work has proved invaluable to my own renderings. I am grateful to Charles Perry and Geert Jan van Gelder for their emergency assistance in identifying an obscurely described party food. Geert Jan also helped to rectify several errors in the reprinting of this translation. Amy Richlin, professor of classics at UCLA, has spent so much time helping me in general that she must surely have facilitated this project in some way. Although this translation would never have happened without the instruction of those people mentioned above, any errors are solely my own.

Mary Selden Evans of Syracuse University Press has patiently corresponded with me and negotiated on my behalf for the past five years, and I would like to express my gratitude to her for her unflagging support for this project. I would also like to thank Annette Wenda for her meticulous and friendly copyediting of this translation, as well as Michael Beard, Kelly Balenske, Marcia Hough, Kay Steinmetz, Hannah Albarazi, Katie Laurentiev, Brooke Carey, and my anonymous reviewers.

Finally, I must thank my family, who have always encouraged me in every way. My brother Matthew painstakingly edited a former introduction to this work, which does not appear in this volume—just one example of his constant love and support. My brother Ben always made me laugh, and probably crashed some parties himself in his day. I dedicate this translation to my parents, who allowed me to follow my interests wherever they may lead.

SELECTIONS FROM

The Art of Party-Crashing
in Medieval Iraq

Al-Khatib al-Baghdadi's Introduction

May God busy us both in obedience to Him, and may He hold you under His protection.

You mentioned to me that you happened to hear about a party-crasher who came to converse with Nasr ibn 'Ali al-Jahdami, and that you wanted to study the story word for word and to examine it more closely.[1] I told you that it had been related to me as well and by what chain of transmission, but we did not have enough time to fill in the details. So I was asked to write it for you and send it to you, and I thus undertake to collect what I have heard of the stories of party-crashers and accounts

---

1. Al-Khatib is referring to anecdote number 145, which likely proved interesting to him because it involves hadith transmission, his main area of study.

about them, and anecdotes of their conversation and poetry.

Perhaps there were more suitable topics with which I could have occupied my mind; the elaboration of some other subject could have been more appropriate and pressing. But I wanted to oblige your request and answer your questions; it is commanded and needful, a requirement and a duty, for I must ensure your esteem for me, and the purity of your friendship, and the sincerity of your love.

In this book I have gathered for you instances of *tatfil* (party-crashing) and its meaning, the first person nicknamed and known for it, opinions about it, its praise and its condemnation, and stories about people branded as its practitioners—everything that gives the scholar's mind a break from the heavy and the serious, so in perusing it, he can rest his thoughts from his uninterrupted study and hard work.

1

'Ali,[2] may God be pleased with him, said:

> If your minds get tired, just as bodies do, seek out some entertaining information!

2. 'Ali was the prophet Muhammad's cousin.

2

Qasama ibn Zuhayr said:

Resting the mind stimulates the memory.

3

The Prophet gives similar license in a hadith told to us by Abu al-Hasan 'Ali ibn Yahya ibn Ja'far al-Imam of Isfahan, that Abu al-Hasan Ahmad ibn al-Qasim ibn al-Rayyan al-Misri in Basra told us, Tamtam, who is Muhammad ibn Ghalib ibn Harb al-Dabbi, related to us, Abu Hudhayfa told us, Sufyan told us on the authority of Salama ibn Kuhayl, on the authority of al-Haytham ibn Hanash, on the authority of Hanzala the scribe, who said:

> The Prophet, may God bless him and give him peace, was talking about Heaven and Hell, and it was as though we were seeing it with our own eyes, but then one day I left and went home to my family. We were laughing together, and I had a sudden sinking feeling. Then I met Abu Bakr, and said to him, "I've been a hypocrite."
>
> "What do you mean?" he asked.
>
> "I was with the Prophet," I replied, "and he was talking about Heaven and Hell, and it was as though I was seeing it with my own eyes, but

3

then I went home to my family, and we laughed together!"

"I've done the same thing," said Abu Bakr.

I went to the Prophet of God, and I told him what had happened.

"O Hanzala," he said, "were you the same with your family as you are with me, it's true, the angels would bless you in your bed and abroad, but Hanzala, there's a time for this and a time for that!"

4

The best and the greatest people never turn their noses up at a jest—they enjoy hearing it and are cheered when it is mentioned. It is rest for the soul and relaxation for the mind—the ear inclines to hear its tales, for therein lies the pleasure of conviviality.

5

Muhammad ibn al-Husayn ibn al-Fadl al-Qattan told me, Abu Bakr Muhammad ibn al-Hasan ibn Ziyad al-Muqri' al-Naqqash told us that Dawud ibn Wasim told them in Bushanj, Abd al-Rahman, nephew of al-Asma'i, told us on the authority of his uncle:

I recited to Muhammad ibn 'Imran, the judge of Medina, one of the most intelligent people I saw among the Quraysh tribe,

You who ask about my home:
The local inn will do.
The baker comes by every day
but takes no IOU.
I gnaw the bread crusts in my bag
until it hurts to chew.

"Write these verses down for me!" he said.
"God help you," I said. "This isn't for the likes of you!"
"Woe to you!" he replied. "Even high-minded and intelligent people like a good joke!"

6

Abu Nu'aym Ahmad ibn 'Abd Allah ibn Ahmad ibn Ishaq al-Hafiz in Isbahan told us, Ahmad ibn Kamil, the judge, told us in his letter to me, I heard Abu al-'Ayna' say, I heard al-Asma'i say:

Witty tales whet the mind and open the ears.

And by God Almighty, I seek success in the correctness of this work and in this writing, and ask to be excused for whatever errors I may have committed.

5

The Meaning of "Party-Crashing" in the Language and the First Person Named after It

I read under al-Hasan ibn Abu al-Qasim on the authority of Abu al-Faraj 'Ali ibn al-Husayn ibn Muhammad al-Isbahani, al-Hasan ibn 'Ali ibn Zakariyya told me, Abu 'Uthman al-Mazini told us, al-Asma'i told us:

> The *tufayli* [party-crasher] enters a party uninvited. The word is derived from the root *tafala*, which refers to the encroaching darkness of nighttime upon the day.

It is implied that the *tufayli* brings darkness upon the party, for the rest do not know who invited him, or how he got in.

8

Al-Husayn ibn Muhammad ibn Ja'far al-Rafiqi told us in his book, 'Ali ibn Muhammad ibn al-Sari al-Hamdani told us, Ahmad ibn al-Hasan al-Muqri' told us, Muhammad ibn al-Qasim ibn Khallad told us, al-Asma'i told us:

> Someone called a *tufayli* goes to banquets uninvited. They are named after Tufayl, a man from Kufa of the Banu Ghatafan, who went to banquets uninvited. He was called "Tufayl of the grooms and the brides."[1]

9

The Bedouin Arab calls a party-crasher a *ra'ish* or a *warish*, and calls someone who goes to a party of drinkers uninvited a *waghil*.

---

1. The explanations provided in anecdotes 7 and 8 contradict one another, but al-Khatib and his contemporaries often strove less in presenting a single narrative and more in "preserving disagreement—indeed, even accentuating it," as Chase Robinson writes of medieval Arabic historians (*Islamic Historiography*, 73). This translation does not always include similar but different repetitions of the same tale; thus, skipped numbers often represent repeated anecdotes with slight variations in word choice—differences carefully preserved in the original Arabic text.

Imru' al-Qays said:

Today I drink sinless before God,
not as a *waghil* . . . [2]

10

'Ali ibn Abu 'Ali al-Mu'addal told us, Muham-
mad ibn 'Abd al-Rahim al-Mazini told us, 'Ubayd
Allah ibn Ahmad ibn Bakr al-Tamimi told us, 'Abd
Allah ibn Muslim ibn Qutayba told us:

Someone entering a party of feasters uninvited is
called a *warish*, and someone entering a party of
drinkers uninvited is called a *waghil*.

11

Al-Hasan ibn 'Ali al-Jawhari told us, Abu 'Amr
Muhammad ibn al-'Abbas al-Kharraz told us, Abu
Bakr Muhammad ibn al-Qasim ibn Bashshar al-
Anbari told us:

2. Imru' al-Qays (d. ca. 565) was the pre-Islamic author of
some of the most famous works of Arabic poetry, often boast-
ing of his female conquests and his acts of mischief and bravery
in the desert.

He who enters the feast of a party uninvited is called a *warish* and a *warush*. The term *tufayli* is used by the common, and is derived from Tufayl of the Weddings, a man who attended banquets in Kufa uninvited.

12

Abu al-Husayn Muhammad ibn 'Abd al-Wahid ibn 'Ali al-Bazzaz told us, Muhammad ibn 'Imran ibn Musa al-Katib told us, Ahmad ibn 'Isa al-Karkhi told us, al-Harith ibn Abi Usama told us, Abu 'Uthman al-Mazini told us, Abu 'Ubayda related to me:

A man from the Banu Hilal was staying by a well, called in those days "Abu Musa's well," because Abu Musa was the first to dig in that spot, and the site was therefore named after him. It was a regular campsite for the Arabs.

So a man of the Banu Hilal was staying there, and his name was Tufayl ibn Zallal. Whenever he heard that some people were having a gathering, he would go there, and he would eat their food. A party-crasher is called a *tufayli* because of that man.

13

Abu 'Abd Allah al-Husayn ibn Muhammad al-Khali' informed us, Muhammad ibn Ahmad ibn Hammad

9

informed us, al-Husayn ibn al-Qasim al-Kawkabi informed us, Ahmad ibn 'Ubayd informed us, al-Asma'i said:

The first person who party-crashed (*taffala*) was "al-Tufayl ibn Zallal." The first person who sneaked food out of a party (*zalla*) was his father. Party-crashing was named after the son, and sneaking food out was named after his father.[3]

3. *Ibn* means "son of"; thus, the father's name, Zallal, is found in the name of the son (al-Tufayl ibn Zallal).

Early Party-Crashing

Abu al-Hasan Muhammad ibn Ahmad ibn Rizq al-Bazzaz told us, Abu Jaʻfar Muhammad ibn Yahya ibn ʻUmar ibn ʻAli ibn Harb al-Taʻi told us, ʻAli ibn Harb told us, Sufyan told us on the authority of ʻAsim ibn Abu al-Nujud,

or

Abu al-Husayn ʻAli ibn Muhammad ibn ʻAbd Allah ibn Bashran al-Muʻaddal told us a number of times, Muhammad ibn ʻAmr ibn al-Bakhtari al-Razzaz told us, Saʻdan ibn Nasr ibn Mansur Abu ʻUthman al-Bazzaz told us, Sufyan ibn ʻUyayna al-Hilali told us on the authority of ʻAsim, on the authority of Zirr, who said, ʻAbd Allah said:

Give lunch to the knowing or the learned, but do not give lunch to the "He's-with-me."

This is the end of the report of 'Ali ibn Harb, but Sa'dan adds, Sufyan said, Abu al-Za'ra' said, on the authority of Abu al-Ahwas, who said, 'Abd Allah said:

In the days before Islam we called someone invited to a party, who brought someone uninvited along with him, a "He's-with-me."[1]

15

'Ubayd Allah ibn Ahmad ibn 'Uthman al-Sayrafi told me, 'Ali ibn 'Umar ibn Ahmad al-Hafiz told us, Abu Rawq al-Hamadhani told us ibn Basra, Bahr ibn Nasr told us in Mecca, 'Abd Allah ibn Wahb told us, and he said, I heard Sufyan al-Thawri said, Abu al-Za'ra' told us on the authority of Abu al-Ahwas on the authority of 'Abd Allah, and he said:

In the pre-Islamic time they considered the "He's-with-me," the one who is invited to a feast and is accompanied by another person, as well as the one whose beliefs are loaded on with others'.

Al-Khatib said:

1. The original Arabic word is *imma'a*, seemingly a contraction of "He is with him."

This means one who makes his beliefs conform to those of other men without looking at the evidence or seeking proof. It is derived from the saddle load that hangs on a horse, for likewise this man hangs the issues of his beliefs on others, relying on imitation rather than striving in his own mind.

19

Al-Hasan ibn Abu Bakr told us, ‘Abd al-Malik ibn al-Hasan al-Mu‘addal told us, Abu Yusuf al-Qadi told us, Sulayman ibn Harb told us, Hammad ibn Salama told us on the authority of Thabit, on the authority of Anas:

> One of the Prophet's neighbors was a Persian, and he made stew that was the most wonderful-smelling thing. One day he was making some food, and went over to the Prophet, who had ‘A'isha by his side, and beckoned for him to come eat. "Can she come with me?" asked the Prophet of God, pointing at ‘A'isha.
>
> "No," said the man.
>
> He pointed at ‘A'isha again and said, "Can she come with me?"
>
> "No," said the man.
>
> He pointed at her a third time and said, "Can she come with me?"

The man said, "Yes," and so 'A'isha went with him.[2]

21

'Ali ibn Muhammad ibn 'Abd Allah ibn Bashran al-Mu'addal told us, Muhammad ibn 'Amr al-Razzaz told us, Muhammad ibn 'Abd Allah ibn Yazid told us, Wahb ibn Jarir told us, Shu'ba told us on the authority of al-A'mash on the authority of Abu Wa'il, on the authority of Abu Mas'ud that:

A man of Medina named Abu Shu'ayb invited the Prophet to come over and to bring five friends. The Prophet sent word back to him asking, "May I bring six?"

The man said that he could.

23

Abu al-Hasan 'Ali ibn Yahya ibn Ja'far al-Isbahani told us, Abu al-Qasim Sulayman ibn Ahmad ibn Ayyub al-Tabarani told us, 'Amr ibn Thawb al-Judhami told us, Muhammad ibn Yusuf al-Firyabi told

2. 'A'isha was the prophet Muhammad's favorite wife.

us, Sufyan told us on the authority of al-A'mash, on the authority of Abu Wa'il, on the authority of Abu Mas'ud:

> We knew a man named Abu Shu'ayb, who had a butcher-slave, and he said to this butcher, "Bring me some food because I want to invite the Prophet over."
>
> He invited the Prophet as the fifth of five guests, but a man followed them to the meal.
>
> The Prophet said to the host, "You invited me as the fifth of five, but this sixth one followed me. If you'd like, give him permission, but if not, he'll go back."
>
> "But I give him permission," the host said.

25

This story was also transmitted on the authority of al-A'mash, Abu Mu'awiya al-Darir, Abu 'Awana, 'Ali ibn Mushir, Yazid ibn 'Ata', 'Abd Allah ibn Dawud al-Harbi, 'Abd Allah ibn Numayr al-Harifi, and Zuhayr ibn Mu'awiya, and they all agree on the chain of transmission as given in the account of Sufyan, which we mentioned above, except for 'Abd Allah ibn Numayr, who said that it was on the authority of Abu Mas'ud, on the authority of Abu Shu'ayb, making it one of those transmitted by Abu Shu'ayb on the authority of the Prophet.[3]

26

As for the hadith of Abu Mu'awiya Muhammad ibn Khazim, Abu Bakr Ahmad ibn 'Ali ibn Muhammad al-Yazdi al-Hafiz told it to us in Naysabur, Abu 'Amr Muhammad ibn Ahmad ibn Hamdan told us, Ibn Shirawayh told us,

or

Abu Bakr al-Baraqani told it to us, saying I read 'Ali 'Abd Allah ibn Muhammad ibn Ziyad saying, 'Abd Allah ibn Muhammad ibn Shirawayh related to you, Ishaq told us, meaning Ibn Ibrahim al-Hanzili, Abu Mu'awiya told us, al-A'mash told us on the authority of Shaqiq on the authority of Mas'ud al-Ansari, who said:

There was one of our men called Abu Shu'ayb, and he said to his slave, "Get me some food, and invite the Prophet of God to come over with whoever is with him."

3. Al-Khatib, a scholar of the hadith, takes special pains with the chains of transmission for these stories about the Prophet. Many of the skipped anecdotes in this early section are repetitions with varying chains of transmission.

The Prophet came and so did those with him, but another man followed who had not been there when they were invited. When the Prophet reached the door, he said to the owner of the house, "A man followed us who was not there when you invited us. If you give him permission, he will come too."

"He has permission," he said. The Prophet of God went in, and the man went in.

28

As for the hadith of 'Ali ibn Mushir, Abu Sa'id al-Hasan ibn Muhammad ibn 'Abd Allah ibn Hasanwayh al-Katib told it to us in Isfahan, Abu Muhammad 'Abd Allah ibn al-Hasan ibn Bundar al-Madini told us, Abu al-Hasan 'Ali ibn Muhammad ibn Sa'id al-Thaqafi al-Kufi told us, al-Minjab ibn al-Harith told us, Ibn Mushir told us on the authority of al-A'mash, on the authority of Shaqiq on the authority of Abu Mas'ud al-Ansari:

One of our men was called Abu Shu'ayb, and he had a butcher-slave. One day he visited the Prophet and saw hunger in his face, so he went to his slave and said, "I have perceived hunger in the face of the Prophet. Make enough food for five, as I would like to invite the Prophet as the fifth of five guests."

17

He made the food, then invited the Prophet of God, but a man followed him.

When the Prophet reached the door, he said, "A man followed us. Do you give him permission, or should he go back?"

"No!" said the host. "Of course I give him permission, Prophet of God!"

Going to a Meal Without Being Invited Is Deemed Rude

33

The judge Abu 'Umar al-Qasim ibn Ja'far ibn 'Abd al-Wahid al-Hashimi told us in Basra, Abu 'Ali Muhammad ibn Ahmad ibn 'Amr al-Lu'lu'i told us, Abu Dawud Sulayman ibn al-Ash'ath told us (or 'Ali ibn Ahmad ibn 'Umar al-Muqri' told us, Muhammad ibn 'Abd Allah al-Shafi'i told us, Mu'adh ibn al-Muthanna told us), and they both said,

Musaddad told us, Durust ibn Ziyad told us on the authority of Aban ibn Tariq, Nafi' related to me in the hadith of Abu Dawud on the authority of Nafi', 'Abd Allah ibn 'Umar said:

The Prophet of God said, "Whosoever receives an invitation and does not respond defies God and his messenger. Whosoever enters a feast uninvited enters a thief and leaves a looter."

This hadith is transmitted only through Nafi' Mawla ibn 'Umar Aban ibn Tariq on the authority of Aban Durust ibn Ziyad.[1]

41

Al-Hasan ibn Abi Bakr told us, Da'laj ibn Ahmad ibn Da'laj al-Mu'addal told us, Musa ibn Harun told us, Abu 'Uthman, who is Sa'id ibn 'Amr, told us, Baqiya told us, Yahya ibn Khalid related to me on the authority of Raw ibn al-Qasim on the authority of al-Maqburi on the authority of 'Urwa on the authority of 'A'isha, and she said:

The messenger of God, peace and prayers upon him, said, "He who enters a party of feasters to which he wasn't invited and eats enters wickedly and eats that which is forbidden."

1. See anecdote 145, in which this hadith and one of its transmitters, Durust ibn Ziyad, become the subject of a heated debate at a party.

45

The judge Abu al-'Ala' Muhammad ibn 'Ali ibn Ya'qub al-Wasiti told us, 'Ali ibn 'Amr ibn Ahmad al-Hafiz told us, Abu al-'Abbas 'Abd Allah ibn Ahmad al-Dimashqi told us, Ibn Ramadan told us, I heard Muhammad ibn 'Abd Allah ibn al-Hakam say:

Eat Dates

I was at al-Shafi'i's house when a man who worked for the police came in. Shafi'i had a plateful of dates in front of him.

The policeman pulled them over and ate every last one.

Then he said, "Hey, Shafi'i! What's your legal opinion on the unexpected guest?"

"You should have asked that question when the dates were still here!" Shafi'i replied.[2]

46

Al-Khatib says:[3]

If a man has a friend whose wife approves of him, and his integrity is not in doubt, then he is allowed to go eat with his friend uninvited, provided that the friend wishes him to, and does not find his presence distasteful, but rather hopes for it.

2. Shafi'i (d. 820) was a famous jurist, after whom was named the Shafi'i branch of Islamic law.
3. Here al-Khatib provides *his* opinion on the unexpected guest, as Shafi'i was too miffed to supply his own in the preceding anecdote.

The origin of that is as Abu Bakr Ahmad ibn 'Umar al-Dallal told us, that 'Abd al-Samad ibn 'Ali ibn Muhammad ibn Mukarram al-Tasti told us by dictation, Ahmad ibn 'Ubayd Allah ibn Idris al-Nursi told us, 'Ubayd Allah ibn Musa told us, Shaban told us on the authority of 'Abd al-Malik ibn 'Umayr on the authority of Abu Salama on the authority of Abu Hurayra:

> The messenger of God went outside at an hour that no one usually goes out and in which you never meet anybody, but then Abu Bakr came up to him.
>
> "What brings you out, Abu Bakr?" he asked him.
>
> "I came out to meet the messenger of God and to look into his face and greet him," he said.
>
> Then, right away, 'Umar came along.
>
> "What brings you out, 'Umar?" he asked.
>
> "I was hungry," he said.
>
> "I find I feel the same way," he replied. "So let's take off to Abu Haytham ibn al-Tayyihan al-Ansari's house!"
>
> He was a man who had a lot of date palms and sheep, but who had no servant. (Then follows the rest of the hadith.)

This hadith relates to the subject of rudeness only in connection to the issue of going to eat uninvited if you're not a true friend, since the host would be grudging in that case.[4]

48

Abu al-Hasan Muhammad ibn Ahmad ibn Rizq al-Bazzaz told us, Abu al-Hasan al-Muzaffar ibn Yahya al-Sharabi told us, Abu al-'Abbas Ahmad ibn Muhammad ibn 'Abd Allah al-Marthadi told us on the authority of Abu Ishaq al-Talhi, Muhammad ibn Ahmad told us, Ibn Abu al-Jarud related that one of his teachers said:

> A wise man told his sons, "Avoid these eight bad habits, for those who exhibit any one of them have only themselves to blame for being despised: a talker who nobody listens to, the one who inserts himself into private matters unasked, the guest at a gathering where he isn't entitled to be, the interloper at an invitation-only party, the petitioner at the door of the stingy, the one seeking aid from his enemy, the one interfering in what does not concern him, and the one who grows foolish over a flirtation."

4. Abu Haytham was indeed a true friend of the Prophet and happily offers him hospitality in the rest of the hadith.

51

'Abd al-Rahman ibn 'Uthman al-Dimashqi wrote to me, and 'Abd al-'Aziz ibn Abi Tahir al-Sufi related to me on his authority, Abu 'Ali al-Hasan ibn Habib al-Faqih told us, Abu Umayya al-Tarsusi told us,

and al-Azhari told us, 'Abd al-Rahman ibn 'Umar told us that Muhammad ibn Ja'far al-Matiri told them, Muhammad ibn Ishaq Abu Bakr al-Saghani told us,

and they both said, Waddah ibn Hassan told us, Abu Hilal al-Rasibi, on the authority of Ghalib al-Qattan, on the authority of Bakr ibn 'Abd Allah:

> The people who most deserve to be slapped are those who come to eat without being invited, and the people who most deserve to be slapped twice are those who, when the host of the party says, "Sit here," reply, "No! I'm going to sit over there!" And the people who most deserve to be slapped three times are those who, when invited to eat, say to the owner of the house, "Call your wife in here to eat with us!"

53

If a guest extends his stay at his host's dwelling until he is driven out, he was party-crashing that house. Tradition has forbidden this.

25

54

Muhammad ibn Ahmad ibn Rizq told us, Abu 'Ali Isma'il ibn Muhammad al-Saffar told us,
   or
The judge Abu Bakr Ahmad ibn al-Hasan ibn Ahmad al-Harashi told us, Abu al-'Abbas Muhammad ibn Ya'qub al-Asamm told us, and they both said, Abu Yahya Zakariyya ibn Yahya al-Marwazi told us, Sufyan told us on the authority of 'Amr, he heard Nafi'a ibn Jubayr tell on the authority of Abu Shurayh al-Khuza'i that the Prophet (peace and prayers upon him) said:

> He who believes in God and the Judgment Day, let him be kind to his neighbor. He who believes in God and the Judgment Day, let him honor his guest. He who believes in God and the Judgment Day, let him speak good or keep silent.

55

Sufyan said, and Ibn 'Ajlan added, on the authority of Sa'id ibn Abi Sa'id, on the authority of his father, on the authority of Abu Shurayh al-Khuza'i, on the authority of the Prophet, peace and prayers upon him:

He who believes in God and the Judgment Day, let him honor his guest, who is allowed a day and a night. Hospitality is for three nights. The guest is not allowed to stay until he is driven out. The host need not spend money on him after that.

Al-Saffar said, "Three nights," and he was reliable.

56

Abu Ya'la Ahmad ibn 'Abd al-Wahid ibn Muhammad al-Wakil told us, Isma'il ibn Sa'id al-Mu'addal told us, al-Husayn ibn al-Qasim al-Kawkabi told us, and he said, Abu al-'Abbas said to us, meaning al-Mubarrad:

A man was staying with a family, and he became a burden to them, so the host asked his wife, "How can we let him know that it's time for him to end his stay here?"

"Let's think up a scheme," she said, "to get him moving."

They thought of one.

The wife asked their guest, "By the One who will surely bless your departure this morning, which of us do you think is the most unjust?"

27

"By the One who will bless my staying with you for a month," said the guest, "I haven't decided yet."

57

Ahmad ibn ʿAli ibn Muhammad al-Muhtasib told us, ʿAbd Allah ibn Muhammad ibn Ahmad al-Muqri' told us, Jaʿfar ibn Muhammad ibn al-Qasim told us, Ahmad ibn Muhammad al-Tusi told us, Ibrahim ibn al-Junayd told us, al-Zubayr ibn Bakkar told us, my uncle Musʿab related to me:

A man from Basra visited a Medinese man who was a friend of his. The Medinese man began to get annoyed by the length of his friend's visit, so one day he said to his wife, "When tomorrow comes, I'm going to ask our guest, 'How many arm's lengths can you jump?' Then I'll jump from the stoop to the gate of the house. When our guest jumps too, I'll close the gate behind him."

The next day the host said, "How's your jumping, Mr. So-and-So?"

"Good," the guest replied.

The host leaped from inside his house to the outside by three arm's lengths.

"Now you jump," he said.

The guest leaped toward the inside of the house by two arm's lengths.

"I jumped outside the house three arm's lengths, and you jumped inside the house only two arm's lengths," said the host.

"Two inside is better than four out!" the guest replied.

Those Who Cast Aspersions on Party-Crashing and Its Practitioners and Satirize and Denounce Them

58

Al-Hasan ibn Abu Bakr told us, Muhammad ibn 'Abd Allah ibn Ibrahim al-Shafi'i told us, Muhammad ibn Ghalib told us, Yahya ibn Isma'il al-Wasiti told us, Mu'tamir ibn Sulayman told us, Qurra related to me on the authority of Muhammad, Ibn 'Umar quotes this line:

> He loves the wine that his friends buy him,
> and hates to part with his own cash!

60

Muhammad ibn al-Hasan ibn 'Ubayd Allah al-Bazzaz recited this to me about one of them:

He thinks of party-crashing as religion,
his only love's to overtake a feast,
and when his hand has seized upon a smidgen,
he halves the loot between his hand and teeth.

61

Abu al-Fath Mansur ibn Rabiʻa ibn Ahmad al-Zuhri,
the preacher in al-Dinawar, told us, Adam al-Tawil
related to me:

> A man came into my tavern for something to eat,
> and a beggar came in behind him.
>
> "You come here so often!" I said to the
> beggar.
>
> "Maybe," said the stranger in the tavern, "he
> is like the one that the poet described:
>
> If pots were cooking underneath the ground,
> or in a distant palace dungeon found,
> and you in China, still you'd find the spot,
> O knower of all hidden things (in pots!)."

64

Muhammad ibn ʻAli ibn al-Hasan al-Jallab recited
this poem to me about a party-crasher:

> More prone to pop in than a fly is,
> to prey on the food and the drink.

If he saw a loaf in the skies,
he'd soar with the birds in a blink!

67

I read this, written by our friend Muhammad ibn Muhammad ibn Zayd al-'Alawi for a litterateur:

He's fond of anyone who throws a party;
he's always at a party in his dreams,
for party-crashing's blazoned on his heart,
a prisoner to the path of fine cuisine.

69

Also 'Ali ibn Abi 'Ali recited this to me on the authority of his father, regarding another one of them:

More pushy than nightfall, and faster . . .
if he's in the house, he's the master!

70

Al-Husayn ibn Muhammad al-Khali' informed us, Abu al-Faraj 'Ali ibn al-Husayn al-Isbahani told us, al-Matiri told us, 'Abd Allah ibn Abu Sa'd told us, Yahya ibn Khalifa al-Darimi related to us, Muhammad ibn Salama related to us, saying:

> A daughter of Musawir the bookseller died on a hot day, and his neighbors didn't come to his assistance. All except kindred avoided him until the weather cooled off.
>
> At last she was borne away. A crowd of his neighbors had followed, so the bookseller turned around and said,

> You didn't help me in my time of need,
> and every party-crasher was abed,
> so quick to come, if coming just to feed,
> so slow to show for carrying the dead!

71

Muhammad ibn al-Hasan ibn 'Ubayd Allah al-Bazzaz recited this to 'Ali ibn al-'Abbas ibn Jurayj al-Rumi concerning the eating habits of party-crashers:

> He fights with friends unless a table joins them,
> and then he's like a serpent at the ball.
> He'll crush rocks with his teeth and never ruin
>   them,
> and on his own he'll outconsume them all,

for should the all-consuming Hell employ him,
it too would bow before his mighty jaw.

73

Muhammad ibn 'Ali ibn 'Ubayd Allah al-Karkhi
recited one of their poems to me:

Whether the rest came early or came late,
he comes right when the cook's about to serve.
The other guests are chastened by his tongue
so sharp the host himself has lost his nerve!

74

Abu 'Abd Allah al-Husayn ibn Muhammad ibn al-
Qasim al-'Alawi recited to me from one of the poems
of Jahza satirizing a singer:

You've gone beyond in party-crashing,
further than we've seen done:
you eat what you oughtn't and then take home
your sugar mama some!

75

Abu Bakr 'Abd Allah ibn 'Ali ibn Hamawayh al-
Hamadhani told us, Ahmad ibn 'Abd al-Rahman

al-Shirazi told us, I heard Abu al-'Abbas Ahmad ibn
Sa'id ibn Ma'dan say, I heard Abu al-Hasan Muhammad ibn Abi Khurasan say, I heard al-'Amri say, I
heard:

Al-Jahiz said,[1] "We knew a young man who was
in love with a concubine. One day he wrote her a
note saying, 'Would that I could sacrifice myself
for you! Send me some sweets and pastries,
because I'm having some Qur'an reciters over.'

"She sent some to him.

"The next day he wrote her another note
saying, 'Would that I could sacrifice myself for
you! Send me some date wine and whatever food
goes well with it, because I'm having some singing slaves over.'

"'May God preserve and extend your life,'
she wrote back, 'I thought that love comes from
the heart, and when it grows serious spreads to
the joints. But your love never left the stomach!
I think you're just a party-crasher, eaten up with
love!'"

1. Al-Jahiz (d. 868–69) was the most famous writer of
classical Arabic prose. He introduced "high" literature to
"low" or "unpoetic" subject matter, like party-crashing, and
was the first to compose a book on the subject, but that manuscript is not extant.

Those Who Praise, Make Excuses for, or Speak Well of Party-Crashing

76

Abu al-Qasim 'Ubayd Allah ibn Ahmad al-Sayrafi and Abu Ya'la Ahmad ibn 'Abd al-Wahid al-Wakil told us, and they said, Muhammad ibn Ja'far al-Tamimi told us, Abu Bakr ibn al-Anbari told us, Tha'lab told us on the authority of Abu Nasr, Al-Asma'i said:

> A Bedouin Arab was listening in on a conversation, and he asked, "Who are these 'party-crashing' people?"
>
> "They are people who come to eat without an invitation," somebody explained.
>
> "By God," he said, "those are some friendly people!"

77

Muhammad ibn 'Ali ibn al-Hasan al-Jallab related to us:

> A man said to his father who was sponging, "O Dad, aren't you ashamed of party-crashing?"
>
> "What do you have against it?" he replied. "Were the children of Israel not sponging when they said, 'Send us, O Lord, a banquet from Heaven that we may have a celebration!'?"[1]

78

Al-Husayn ibn Muhammad ibn Ja'far al-Rafiqi informed us that, 'Ali ibn Muhammad ibn al-Sari told us, Ahmad ibn al-Hasan al-Muqri' told us:

> Someone told Bunan, "Someone who enters a meal uninvited enters a thief and leaves a looter!"
>
> "I've never eaten anything that wasn't allowed," he replied.
>
> "How's that?" someone asked.
>
> "Doesn't the host of the banquet say to the cook, 'Make too much of everything. If we want

---

1. This is a verse from the Qur'an chapter "The Table-Spread" (5:114).

to serve a hundred, make enough for a hundred and twenty, because we'll get some guests we expected and some we didn't'?

"Well, I'm one of the ones they didn't expect!" said Bunan.[2]

79

Abu Bakr Ahmad ibn Sulayman ibn 'Ali al-Muqri' told us, 'Ubayd Allah ibn Muhammad al-Bazzaz told us, Ja'far ibn Muhammad ibn al-Qasim told us, Abu al-'Abbas al-Tusi told us, Muhammad ibn Sa'id told us:

I once said to a party-crasher, "Woe unto you! You eat what is forbidden!"

"I've never eaten a bite that wasn't allowed," he replied.

"How's that?" I asked.

"Because when I go into a party, I head for the door to the women's quarters, and everyone says, 'No, not there! Here! Here!' Their saying 'Here!' *is* the invitation, so therefore I don't eat anything that isn't allowed."

2. Bunan was a famous party-crasher, featured in a later chapter of this translation.

80

Abu al-Qasim al-Azhari told me, Ahmad ibn Ibrahim told us, 'Ubayd Allah ibn 'Abd al-Rahman al-Sukkari told us, 'Abd Allah ibn Abi As'ad told us, Ahmad ibn Jabir ibn Yazid related to me, Sindi ibn Sadaqa related to me, and he said:

> We were on a roof (in Egypt, I mean), and Abu Nuwas was with us.[3] A group passed by on their way to al-Khasib, and Abu Nuwas called for an inkstand and wrote to them:

> You have invited a group to go;
> another group would like to crash.
> They hope you'll take the crashing well,
> for hope's, you know, a stronghold vast.
> Receive them, please, you gentlemen,
> as kindly now as in the past!

81

Ahmad ibn Muhammad ibn 'Abd al-Wahid al-Munkadiri recited this to me, on Abu Rawh Zafar ibn 'Abd Allah al-Harawi:

---

3. Abu Nuwas (d. 813) is perhaps the most famous of classical Arabic poets, known especially for his homoerotic verses and his wine poetry.

A party-crasher's dear to me,
as dear as my own friends,
he comes without an invite,
and a new friendship begins.
For all the people, near and far,
my table's always set . . .
I may neglect to call them all,
but crashers don't forget!

82

Abu Talib 'Amr ibn Ibrahim ibn Sa'id al-Zuhri al-Faqih told me, Muhammad ibn al-'Abbas al-Khazzaz told us, and he said, Muhammad ibn 'Abd Allah al-Katib recited to us, Muhammad ibn al-Marzubani recited to us, and he said, I recited one of the secretary's poems:

To him who daily blames us party-crashers:
I take my brothers' banquets up with zeal!
What speech is more delicious or more dear
than conversation 'round a common meal?

83

Muhammad ibn al-Hasan ibn Ahmad al-Ahwazi recited to me, saying, al-Walid ibn Ma'an al-Mawsili recited to us, saying, I recited one of their poems:

Continue, pleasures of *Tatfil*,
persist and never leave!
For you can cure what ails me,
and you can heal my grief!

Party-Crashers from among the Notables, the Noble, the Learned, and the Cultured

85

Al-Hasan ibn Abu Bakr told me, Abu al-Fadl 'Isa ibn Musa ibn Abu Muhammad ibn al-Mutawakkil 'Ali Allah told us, Muhammad ibn Khalaf ibn al-Marzuban said, al-'Abbas ibn Hisham told this story on the authority of his brother Unayf ibn Hisham, who heard it from his father, who heard it from someone from Medina, who said:

'Abd Allah ibn Ja'far and a number of his friends passed the house of a man who had just gotten married.[1]

1. 'Abd Allah ibn Ja'far (d. 699) was "the most generous man in Islam." *Tatfil* (1999), 83n. He also has the honor of

When they passed, suddenly a singing-girl said,

Tell the noblemen there at the door to come in—
to behave like a child while you're young is no sin!

"Go in," 'Abd Allah said to his friends. "We were just invited to the party."

So he got off his horse, and his friends got off as well, and they went in. When the owner of the house saw the arrivals, he seated them all on a mat.

"How much did you pay for your banquet?" 'Abd Allah asked the man.

"A hundred dinars," he said.

"And how much was your dowry?" he asked.

The man told him the amount.

'Abd Allah ordered a hundred dinars and the amount of the man's dowry to be given to him, along with a hundred extra dinars to back it up. Then he apologized and departed.

86

Al-Hasan ibn al-Husayn ibn al-'Abbas al-Ni'ali told us, Abu al-Faraj 'Ali ibn al-Husayn al-Isbahani told

---

being the only party-crasher in this collection with a guilty conscience.

us, Ahmad ibn 'Abd al-'Aziz told us, al-Hasan ibn
'Ali related to me, 'Ali ibn Sa'id al-Kindi told us, I
heard Abu Bakr 'Ayyash say:

> I was told that Dhu al-Rumma was a party-
> crasher who went to weddings.[2]

87

Abu Sa'id Muhammad ibn Musa ibn al-Fadl ibn
Shadhan al-Sayrafi told us, I heard Abu al-'Abbas
Muhammad ibn Ya'qub al-Asamm say, I heard al-
'Abbas ibn Muhammad al-Duri say, I heard Yahya
ibn Ma'in say:

> Zakariyya ibn Manzur was a party-crasher.[3]

88

'Ali ibn al-Muhassin al-Tanukhi told us, I found
written in a book of my grandfather, Harami ibn

---

2. Dhu al-Rumma was a nickname for Ghaylan ibn
'Uqba, a famous poet who lived in the eighth century.
3. Zakariyya ibn Manzur was a transmitter of hadith
whose transmissions were not considered trustworthy. Ibid.,
84n.

Abi al-'Ala' told us, Ishaq ibn Muhammad ibn Aban al-Nakha'i told us, al-Qahdhami related to me:

> Raqaba would sit in the mosque, and when he left in the evening he would seek out some table companions in the houses neighboring the mosque. He would visit every man of them in their houses one after another, and he would eat.
>
> "Would that the nighttime would last and last, until the Day of Resurrection!" he would say.[4]

89

Abu Talib Muhammad ibn al-Husayn ibn Ahmad ibn 'Abd Allah ibn Bukayr told us, the judge Abu Hamid Ahmad ibn al-Husayn ibn 'Ali al-Hamadhani told us, Ahmad ibn al-Harith ibn Muhammad ibn 'Abd al-Karim told us, my grandfather Muhammad ibn 'Abd al-Karim al-'Abdi told us, al-Haytham ibn 'Adi told us:

> Raqaba ibn Masqala al-'Abdi went to see Mis'ar ibn Kidam and threw himself on his back.
>
> "What's the matter?" Mis'ar asked him.

---

4. Raqaba was a trusted hadith transmitter who also liked jokes. Ibid., 85n.

"I've been struck down by *faludhaj*,"[5] he said. "We were in a man's house who was acting as a judge for a group of people, and arbitrating between the disagreeing parties, and Walid ibn Harb ibn al-Harith ibn Abu Musa al-Ash'ari invited us to a banquet. They produced a table as big as a crater. Then they produced thin bread that was like an elephant's ears, and then watercress like the ears of a goat, and then smooth stew and a water-dweller with a back like the back of a *qirati* bird, and then we were given *faludhaj* so transparent you could read the inscription of a coin through it. He topped it all off with a giant jug, and we were in rapture about this and certain that we would all get some of that."

"Hey," said Mis'ar, who was nicknamed Abu Salama, "do you think you're becoming a sponger?"

"Hey, 'Pop,'" he replied (that was how they addressed one another), "they're all spongers, though they hide it from one another."

91

I read one of their poems in our friend Muhammad ibn Muhammad ibn Zayd al-'Alawi's book:

5. *Faludhaj* is a pastry made from almonds and sugar.

If you know what's polite, don't blame me
    outright.
I'm alone in my house while you're drinking all
    night;
The apostle approves writing my own invite!

92

Ahmad ibn 'Ali ibn al-Husayn al-Tawwazi told us, 'Ubayd Allah ibn Muhammad ibn Ahmad al-Muqri' told us, Ja'far ibn al-Qasim told us, Ahmad ibn Muhammad al-Tusi told us, Ibn Abu Sa'd told us, 'Umar ibn Isma'il ibn 'Abd al-'Aziz ibn 'Umar ibn 'Abd al-Rahman ibn 'Awf related to us, Muhammad ibn Shafana al-Ghifari related to me:

Hakam al-Wadi the singer left Wadi, having quarreled with his father, and went on until he reached Medina. There he befriended a group of camel drivers and assisted them on their journey to Kufa, riding with them on the trail until they entered the city. Then he asked them,

"Who can tell me who in Kufa drinks wine and entertains friends at home?"

"So-and-So the cloth merchant," someone replied. "He has drinking companions who are also cloth merchants, and all these merchants go to one of their houses every day. When it's Friday, they all go to his house."

So Hakam al-Wadi went out and joined their circle, each one of the guests thinking that he had come with someone else. They talked with him and he with them until they departed.

So when they went to the cloth merchant's house, al-Wadi was with them.

As the gathering got started, a concubine came out and took their cloaks and folded them. They were brought food, and then they were brought wine, and they drank, all still thinking that al-Wadi was one of them, until they became cheerful and the wine went to their heads. Then al-Wadi got up to go to the toilet. The remaining guests turned to one another and said, "Who did he come with?"

"By God, I don't know!" everyone said.

"A party-crasher," they concluded.

"But don't say anything," said the owner of the house, "because he is high-minded and of agreeable intelligence."

Al-Wadi heard what they said.

When he came back out, he greeted the crowd, then asked the owner of the house, "Is there a square tambourine around?"

"No, by God!" said the host. "But we'll get one for you." He sent someone out to the market to purchase one. The other guests gathered that he was a musician.

The moment the tambourine fell into his hands and he shook it, it almost spoke. The crowd almost soared from pleasure as he smacked the tambourine. Then he sang from his throat, and none of them had heard anything like it before. When he fell silent, they said, "By my father! It couldn't have been done any better."

"I heard what you said," he replied, "when you mentioned party-crashing. Why do you have a problem with somebody going into a party with you?"

"It doesn't matter to us one bit," they said.

He spent the whole day with them.

"Where were you intending to go?" they asked him.

"To the Commander of the Faithful's door," he replied.

"How much were you hoping he would give you?" they asked.

"A thousand dinars," he replied.

"We swear before God," they said, "that you will not have an audience with the prince, and he will not see you, for you will see no other country but Kufa, and the thousand dinars are on us." Then they gathered together a thousand dinars among them, as well as clothing for his family and his father, and presents from Iraq. He stayed with them until he began to miss his family, and then they provided him with transportation, and he returned home.

93

Muhammad ibn ʿAli ibn ʿAbd Allah al-Suri related to me, ʿAbd al-Rahman ibn ʿUmar al-Tujibi in Egypt told us, Abu Hurayra Ahmad ibn ʿAbd Allah ibn al-Hasan ibn Abu al-ʿAssam al-ʿAdawi told us, Abu al-ʿAbbas ʿIsa ibn ʿAbd al-Rahim told us, ʿAli ibn Muhammad who is the son of Hayyun related to me, Muhammad ibn Ahmad al-Kufi related to me, al-Husayn ibn ʿAbd al-Rahman of Aleppo related to me that his father said that:

> Once al-Maʾmun heard of ten heretics among the people of Basra and commanded that they be brought to him. They were being gathered together when a party-crasher caught sight of the group and said, "What could they possibly be gathered for except a feast!" He slipped into their midst, and the guards herded them along to the prison boat.
>
> "A pleasure cruise!" the party-crasher said, and got on the boat with the rest. It wasn't a moment before they were all in shackles, the party-crasher included. "Look what my party-crashing has amounted to!" he said. "Shackles!"
>
> They reached Baghdad and were taken to al-Maʾmun,[6] who made them call out their names,

6. Al-Maʾmun was the Abbasid caliph from 813 to 833, two hundred years before al-Khatib al-Baghdadi's time.

man by man. Then he ordered that their necks be struck until he reached the party-crasher, who was at the end of the line.

"Who is this?" al-Ma'mun asked the guards.

"By God, we don't know!" they said. "We just found him tagging along, so we brought him with us!"

Al-Ma'mun looked at the party-crasher and said, "Damn it, what's your story!?"

"O Commander of the Faithful!" he cried. "May he who has any idea what these people were claiming divorce his wife! As for me, I don't know anything but God and the prophet Muhammad, prayers and peace upon him. . . . I'm just a guy who saw these people in a group, and I thought they were going somewhere to eat!"

Al-Ma'mun laughed and said, "Let him be punished."

Ibrahim ibn al-Mahdi,[7] who was in al-Ma'mun's court at the time, said, "O Commander

---

This story also appears in the "Barber's Tale" in the *1001 Nights*.

7. Ibrahim ibn al-Mahdi (d. 839) was the son of the caliph al-Mahdi and briefly the successor of al-Ma'mun. He was ill-suited to political life because of his consuming passion for singing and music, and he spent his later years as a court poet and musician. D. Sourdel, *The Encyclopaedia of Islam* (1971), s.v. "Ibrāhīm ibn al-Mahdī."

of the Faithful, let me take the burden of his punishment by telling you a wondrous account about myself!"

So he said, "Speak, Ibrahim."

"Commander of the Faithful!" began Ibrahim. "Once I went riding out of your palace just for fun, and started down a side lane with a wall at the end. There I smelled, O King, a whiff of spices, the aroma spreading so deliciously.

"I longed for it because of its scrumptious scent, so I stopped by the tailor's house and asked him, 'Do you know who lives in that house?'

"'A man who is a cloth merchant,' he said.

"'What's his name?' I asked him, and he said 'So-and-So.'

"So I walked around the side of the house where there were some windows, and I saw a lady put her hand out of the window, all the way past the wrist to the upper arm.

"And I was mesmerized, O Commander of the Faithful, more by the beauty of the hand and the wrist than by the aroma of the stew. I lingered a long while before regaining my senses.

"Then I asked the tailor, 'Does So-and-So drink wine?'

"'Yes,' said the tailor. 'In fact, I think he's having a little gathering today, but he's just drinking with some merchants like him.'

"Just then I saw two noble men riding down the alley, and the tailor said, 'Those are the people he invited.' I asked him what their names were and he said, 'So-and-So and So-and-So.'

"So I got back on my horse and rode up to the men, saying, 'So-and-So! May I be your ransom! I've been waiting for you! May God hold you dear!' And I kept up like that until we reached the door, at which point they did me the honor of letting me go in first. I went in and they went in, and when the owner of the house saw me with them, he didn't doubt that I was their friend, or that I had met them somewhere, so he welcomed me and put me at the best place at the table.

"And then, O Commander of the Faithful, they brought wonderful bread to the table, and gave us all kinds of food, which was even more delicious than the aroma that I had smelled. And I thought to myself, 'I've now tasted their food, but what of that hand and its owner?'

"Then the meal was lifted away and the washing bowl was brought out, and we all went into the drinking room. I don't know if I've ever seen a nicer household, O King, and the owner fawned over me and made kind conversation with me, so that nobody doubted he had known me for a long time, because everybody just assumed that I was one of them.

"When we were drinking from the wine goblets, a concubine came out. O King! She was like a bending willow branch, and she approached and greeted us, not at all shy, and she gathered

up a cushion and sat down. An oud was brought
out and placed in her lap, and she tested it gently
so that I could tell by her testing that she was a
skillful player. Then she plunged into a song:

My gaze rose warm as the sun on her cheek
and dawned as a tenuous blush,
her hand and her fingertips trembling and weak
from my heartbeat's palpable touch.

"And she stirred in me, O King, a great uneasi-
ness, and I was overwhelmed by the beauty of her
poetry and her skill.
      "She then plunged into a song:

My eyes addressed her, made her know.
Her eyes replied, 'I'm taken, though!'
I turned my eyes in silence so
her eyes grew silent, quid pro quo.

"'Oh!' I cried, Commander of the Faithful, because of her skill. I was so transported that I could
hardly control myself, and then she plunged into
a third song:

Is it not wondrous that a poem enfolds me?
But we are not alone: beware of speech!
. . . and yet your eyes are eloquently sightly
and broken sighs as well as flutes beseech,

the lips give sign, the eyebrows signal lightly,
the eyelids and the hand wave, each to each.

"I envied her talent, O Commander of the Faithful, and the wounding meaning of her poetry, and that she hadn't made good the promise implied in her art, so I leered, 'God preserve you, concubine,' and she smacked the floor with her oud and said to the others, 'Since when do you spend time with boors like this?'

"Then I regretted what I had done, and I saw the crowd's attitude toward me was starting to change, so I said, 'Isn't there an oud here?'

"'Of course there is,' they said, and gave me the oud. So I adjusted it to my liking, and I plunged into a song:

Why do these campsites not answer the
    grieving?
Perhaps they are deaf, or petrified.
Their inhabitants left one remembered
    evening—
I live if they live. I die if they've died.

"And I had hardly finished, O Commander of the Faithful, when the concubine leaped up, leaned over, and kissed my feet! 'O my lord,' she said penitently. 'By God, I've never heard anyone sing that song like you!' And her master leaped up and everybody who was there, and they all exclaimed as she had, and the entire crowd was overjoyed and encouraged to quaff their wine in goblets and draughts.[8] Then I plunged into a song:

Is it God's will your eyes don't recognize me
while memory leaves in mine a bloody stain?
I cry to God I gave my love like honey
while giving seems to you a bitter strain.
Return the mangled heart you murdered to me!
Leave not the madman standing in a flame!
I cry to God you are a stranger to me,
a stranger to this land of loving pain.

"The excitation of the crowd was so extreme, O Commander of the Faithful, that I was afraid they might go out of their heads. So I restrained myself for a while, trying to calm their passion. But then they plunged into drink in earnest, intent on that passion, and once again I plunged into a song:

8. As the most recent editor of this text, al-Jabi, notes, in earlier editions all mention of wine is removed from this and other stories. He strongly condemns this act of censorship (*Tatfil*, 93n). Van Gelder calls modern attempts to deny the presence of alcohol consumption in medieval Arabic literature "naïve and disingenuous" (*Of Dishes and Discourse*, 69).

Behold your lover infolded in grief
awash in a river of crying,
One of his hands is beseeching his Lord,
and one on his liver is lying.[9]
Read in the lines of his hands and his eyes
the destiny, dear, of the dying!

"Then the concubine started crying, 'My God, what a song, my lord!' and the crowd was intoxicated and out of their heads, and the owner of the house was extremely liberal with his drink. But he was prudent and ordered two of his slaves to help the slaves of his guests support them and conduct them back to their houses.

"So I was left alone with him, drinking goblets of wine, until he said to me, 'My friend! All the days that I didn't know you were days wasted! Who are you, my lord?' And he wouldn't let off beseeching until I told him. Then he leaped up and kissed my head and said, 'Of course! I doubt that anyone but you could play the oud like that. If I were from the royal court, wouldn't I be eloquent too?!'

"Then he asked me my story, and how I came to do what I had done, so I told him about

9. The word *liver* is used to indicate the emotional core of the body, like *heart* in English poetry.

the food, and about the hand and the wrist that I
saw reaching from the window, and I said, 'As for
the food, it fulfilled my desires . . . ,' and he said,
'What about the hand and the wrist?'

"Then he said, 'Hey, So-and-So!' to one of
his concubines, and made her come over, and he
made all his concubines come over to me one
by one and show me their hands and wrists, but
each time I said, 'It isn't she.'

"Finally, he said, 'By God, there's nobody
left but my sister and my mother. By God, I'm
going to call them in here for you.'

"I was amazed at his generosity and his big-
heartedness. 'If I could only sacrifice myself for
you!' I exclaimed. 'I'll look at your sister before
your mother, possibly it will be she . . .'

"'You're right,' he said, and she came out.
When I saw her hand and her wrist, I said, 'It
is she.'

"So he ordered his slaves to fetch ten sheikhs
who lived nearby at the time, and when the slaves
brought them, he called for two giant sums of
coin, ten thousand dirhams each. He said to the
sheikhs, 'This is my sister, So-and-So. Bear wit-
ness to the fact that she is now married to Mr.
Ibrahim ibn al-Mahdi.'

"I presented his twenty thousand dirhams to
her as a dowry, and she was pleased and accepted
the marriage. She divided the dowry in half, giving ten thousand to the sheikhs.

Aroma

"Then he said, 'You are excused,' and they left immediately, taking the money with them

"'My friend!' he said to me. 'I'll get one of my dwellings ready for you and your new family to sleep in.' And I was ashamed, for, my God, I'd never seen a man so openhearted and noble natured.

"'I'd rather call a litter and carry her to my house,' I said.

"She said, 'As you like,' so I called a litter, and she was carried to my house.

"By your truth, O King, they even brought us some provisions that we needed, and I who

59

stand before you consummated the marriage without delay."

The Commander of the Faithful was astounded by the generosity and openheartedness of the man, and he said, "May God bless him and his family! I've never heard anything like it!" Then he freed the party-crasher and granted him a wonderful boon, and ordered Ibrahim to fetch the generous man from the story. That man became one of the caliph's dearest companions.

94

'Ali ibn Abu 'Ali al-Basri told me, my father related to me, Abu al-Faraj 'Ali ibn al-Husayn known as al-Isbahani related this story publicly from memory, and I wrote it down with his permission, but I don't have my book with me, so I've recited it from memory.[10] I've struggled to recite it word for word:

Muhammad ibn Ibrahim al-Mawsili told me, my father related to me:[11]

---

10. Abu al-Faraj (al-Isbahani) (d. 967) was the author of the famous *Kitab al-aghani* (The Book of Songs), in which he described famous poets (such as the hero of this anecdote) and their songs.

11. Ibrahim al-Mawsili (d. 904), the narrator of this anecdote, was "one of the greatest musicians and composers of the

I got up one morning, and I was tired of sticking around the caliph's palace and my service there, so I rode out in the morning and decided to take a jaunt in the desert. I set off. I told my slave boys, "If the caliph's messenger or someone else comes, tell them that I went out early on an errand and that you don't know which way I went." Then I took off wandering where I pleased.

When I came back, the day had grown ragingly hot, and I paused to rest on a road in Mukharram. On this road was a densely shaded courtyard, with a spacious outdoor portion in which I settled down for some relaxation.

Before long a servant boy passed by, leading a merry little donkey, and on the donkey was a concubine. Beneath the concubine was a riding handkerchief, and she was wearing a splendid gown—the height of fashion. I could see that she had a noble bearing, a languid gaze, and elegant features, and I surmised that she was a singing-girl.

She entered the house that I was standing in front of, and my heart attached itself to her decisively, so that I couldn't get it free again.

---

early Abbasid period . . . whose melodies were so entrancing that they were ascribed to the inspiration of the Devil himself." J. W. Fück, *The Encyclopaedia of Islam* (1971), s.v. "Ibrāhīm al-Mawsilî, Abû Ishâk." *Ibn* means "son," so Ibrahim's son Muhammad (Ibn Ibrahim al-Mawsili) is the first transmitter of his story.

It was nothing but a moment until two beautiful young men passed the same way. They had a noble demeanor that showed their status, and they were both riding. They asked permission, and permission was granted them to enter.

I was burdened by what love had grown in my heart for the concubine and by my anxiousness for her presence, so I obtained access to her by entering with the two young men. They thought I was invited by the owner of the house; the owner of the house thought that I was with them. Food was brought out, which we ate, and drinks were placed before us. Then the concubine appeared with an oud in her hand, and she seemed to me a beautiful concubine, and what was growing in my heart grew even more. She sang well, and we drank.

I got up to urinate, and the owner of the house asked the two young men about me, and they replied that they did not know me. "This is a party-crasher," he said. But he was gracious, and his company embraced me as one of their number. I came and sat back down, and the concubine sang—one of my own melodies!

Remember the passing of Lady Gazelle?
The riding beasts stirred at the sound and the
    sight.
A belle, her steps written in sand as they fell,
her margins illumined in dawn's first light.

She rendered the song beautifully, and drank. Then she sang more songs, some of which were my own compositions:

Effaced traces, footprints of young girls,
deserted now . . . by brambles overcurled.

And her command of this song was more excellent than the last. Then she sang more melodies, some ancient and some modern, and several of them were my own compositions and my own poetry:

Tell the one who spurns you,
who repels you from his side,
"The one who loves, you love as well;
you're only playing sly!
I here proclaim your cruelty
a pretense and a lie!"

This song was the most exquisite of all, and I begged her to repeat it so that I could make sure she had it right. Then one of the two young men approached me and said, "I've never met a party-crasher more brazen than you—you're not content with crashing our party until you've bossed us around as well! This just proves the saying that party-crashers are bossy." I bowed my head and didn't answer. His friend told him to leave me alone, but he wouldn't let up.

At that point everybody got up to perform the prayers, but I lingered behind. I picked up the concubine's oud and tightened its strings and tuned it properly, then I returned to my place and performed the prayers. Everybody came back. The young man tried to quarrel with me again, but I was silent. The concubine picked up her oud. She tested it, and she could feel that something was different.

"Who touched my oud?" she said.

"Nobody touched it," said the others.

"But yes!" she exclaimed. "By God, somebody skillful has tightened its strings and tuned it in a way exactly appropriate to its design."

Then I said, "I tuned it."

"For Heaven's sake, my lord, take it and play it!" she said.

So I took it from her, and I played it, beginning with a wondrous, difficult passage with some very moving finger-plucking bits, until people from all around had gathered to hear me play.

They said, "For Heaven's sake, my lord! Do you sing as well?"

And I said, "Yes! And I will also tell you who I am: I am Ishaq ibn Ibrahim al-Mawsili, and by God I've come here from the caliph! You have been abusing me all day because I trifled with you on account of this concubine, and by God I won't say another word nor sit with you until you expel that quarrelsome, wretched boor."

I got up to leave and they hung on me, but I refused to turn back. The concubine caught up with me, and she hung on me as well, so I said, "I'm not sitting down unless they expel that quarrelsome, low-life loser!"

His friend said to him, "I warned you not to try anything like this again," and he began to apologize.

"I'll sit," I said, "but by God I won't sing a note with him here." So he took the youth by the hand and led him out. I sang the song of mine that the concubine had sung earlier, and the owner of the house was greatly moved.

"Is there anything of mine that you'd like to have?" he asked.

"Like what?" I asked.

"Stay with me a month, and I'll give you the concubine and the donkey, along with the concubine's wardrobe."

"I'll do it," I said, and stayed with him for thirty days without anybody knowing where I was. Al-Ma'mun asked for me everywhere, but nobody had any news of my whereabouts.

When thirty days had passed, he released the concubine, the donkey, and the servant to me, with whom I returned to my household, which was in a pitiful state owing to my absence. Eventually, I rode to al-Ma'mun, and when he saw me he said, "Ishaq! Damn it, where were you?!"

I told him and he said, "Show me this man immediately!" So I took him to the house. He was home, so al-Ma'mun asked him to tell the story again. He told it, and al-Ma'mun said, "You are a chivalrous man with chivalrous ways."

He ordered that he be given a hundred thousand dirhams, and he said, "Don't associate with that low-life quarrelsome youth anymore."

"God forbid, O King!" said the man.

Singing-Girl

Then al-Ma'mun gave me fifty thousand dirhams and said, "Bring me the concubine."

I brought her, and she sang the caliph a song.

He said to me, "I'd like to put her on a schedule where she sings every Wednesday from behind a screen with the other concubines," and he gave her fifty thousand dirhams. By God, she made a great profit from it too.

95

Ahmad ibn ʿAli ibn al-Husayn al-Tawwazi told me, ʿUbayd Allah ibn Muhammad ibn Ahmad ibn al-Muqriʾ told us, Jaʿfar ibn al-Qasim told us, Ahmad ibn Muhammad al-Tusi told us:

My father related to me that he heard Mukhariq the singer say,[12] "I performed an act of party-crashing that cost the Commander of the Faithful, al-Muʿtasim, a hundred thousand dirhams."

"How'd you do it?" someone asked.

12. Mukhariq (d. 845), originally a slave to the female singer and lutenist ʿAtika bint Shudha, and a student of the famous musician Ibrahim al-Mawsili (of the previous anecdote), was so skilled in singing and playing the oud that the caliph Harun al-Rashid granted him his freedom and made him a favorite of the court. H. G. Farmer, *The Encyclopaedia of Islam* (1993), s.v. "Mukhāriḳ."

He said, "I drank with al-Mu'tasim from dusk to dawn, and when the morning came I said, "My Lord, might the Commander of the Faithful see his way to granting me permission to take a breather in al-Rusafa until he needs me again?"[13]

"Okay," he said. He gave the command to the gatekeepers, and they left me alone.

I began walking in al-Rusafa [said Mukhariq], when I saw a concubine who looked as though the sun were shining from her features, so I followed her.

She had a basket of palm leaves, and she stopped at the fruit seller and bought a quince for a dirham, a pomegranate for a dirham, and a pear for a dirham. I continued following her until she turned around and saw me behind her.

"Stay away, mister!" she said. "Just where do you think you're going?"

"Behind you, my lady," I said.

"Get back, you jerk," she replied. "If anyone sees you, you're dead!"

Then she paused for a bit and looked me over.

Then [said Mukhariq] she abused me twice as much as she had the first time, and she walked to a big door and went inside.

13. Al-Rusafa was a quarter of the city of Baghdad.

I sat outside the door, and I daydreamed, and the sun went down. It was a hot day.

But it wasn't too long before two young men came, looking pretty as a picture, riding on Egyptian donkeys. Permission was granted them to enter, and I went in with them. The owner of the house thought that I came with his friends, and his friends thought that the owner of the house had invited me. Food was presented, and everyone ate and washed their hands. Then the host said, "Would you like to see a girl?"

"If you please," they replied.

The concubine came out, looking straight ahead of her, with a slave girl carrying her oud. She placed the oud on her lap and she sang, and everyone enjoyed themselves and drank.

"Who wrote that song, lady?" everyone asked.

"Mr. Mukhariq wrote it," she replied.

Then she sang another tune, and everyone enjoyed it—they enjoyed it even more than the last one.

"Who wrote that song, lady?" they said.

"Mr. Mukhariq," she replied.

Then she sang a third song, and they enjoyed themselves and drank. Meanwhile, the concubine was glancing at me and feeling suspicious.

"Who wrote that, lady?" they said, and she said, "Mr. Mukhariq."

Then I lost my patience [said Mukhariq], and I said to her, "Concubine! Tighten your grip!"

She tightened her grip, but began to lose her rhythm. I then asked for the oud, and I performed and sang the tune that she had first sung. Everybody leaped up and kissed my head.

[My father said that Mukhariq had the best voice and was great with his "tool."][14]

Then I sang the second and the third songs, and they went wild and nearly lost their minds.

"Who are you, my lord?" they asked.

"I'm Mukhariq!" I said.

"What's your purpose with us?" they asked.

"Party-crashing, God keep you," I replied, and I told them my story.

The owner of the house turned to his two friends. "As you know," he said, "I paid thirty thousand dirhams for that concubine, but she was undervalued by at least ten thousand, and I refuse to sell her for less than forty thousand dirhams."

"We have twenty thousand dirhams each," said the two youths, and they made me her owner.

14. This aside seems to be an interruption of the narrator, Ahmad ibn Muhammad al-Tusi, whose father first heard and related Mukhariq's tale (see the chain of transmission at the beginning of the anecdote).

Meanwhile, al-Muʿtasim was waiting. He had requested me at the commander's sons' house, and I hadn't come, so he was angry with me.

But I stayed with the party for a time, and when I left I took the girl. When we came to the place where she had insulted me, I said to her, "Mistress, take back those insults you said to me," and she conceded and vowed to take them back. I held her hand until we came to the door of the Commander of the Faithful, al-Muʿtasim. I walked in with my hand in hers. When he saw me, he cursed and insulted me.

"Don't be hasty!" I said, and I told him what had happened.

Then he laughed. "I will compensate those men for you, Mukhariq," he said, and commanded that each man be given thirty thousand dirhams, and he gave me ten thousand dirhams.

Those Who Engage in Very Subtle Acts of Party-Crashing

96

Al-Husayn ibn Muhammad ibn al-Hasan al-Mu'addib told us, Isma'il ibn Ahmad al-Kashani told us, Muhammad ibn Yusuf al-Firabri told us, Isma'il ibn al-Bukhari told us, Abu al-Rahman ibn Shayba told us, Ibn Abu Fudayk told me, on the authority of Ibn Abu Dhi'b, on the authority of al-Maqburi, on the authority of Abu Hurayra, who said:

> I was staying close to the Prophet of God in order to fill my belly at a time when I did not eat leavened bread, I did not wear silk, I had neither servant nor maid, I tightened my belt with stones, and I asked men to teach me verses of the Qur'an that I already knew so that they would invite me in and feed me.

Al-Hasan ibn Abi Bakr told me, Abu al-Fadl 'Isa ibn Musa ibn Abi Muhammad ibn al-Mutawakkil 'Ali Allah told me, Ibn Khalaf ibn al-Marzuban told me, Ahmad ibn Mansur related to us, 'Abd Allah ibn Sa'id ibn al-Husayn al-Kindi told us, Isma'il ibn Ibrahim al-Tamimi told us, Ibrahim ibn Ishaq al-Makhzumi told us, on the authority of al-Maqburi:

> Abu Hurayra said, "I used to ask the companions of the Prophet about verses of the Qur'an that I already knew, just so they would feed me something.

Kitten

"Whenever I asked Ja'far ibn Abi Talib about a verse, he would never answer me until he had taken me back to his home and had said to his wife, 'Hey, Asma'! Get us something to eat!' After she had fed us, he would answer me. Ja'far loved his neighbors, and was always sitting with them and sharing hadith with them."[1]

98

Abu Nu'aym al-Hafiz told us, Abu Ishaq Ibrahim ibn Muhammad ibn Hamza told us, Abu Ya'la (who is al-Mawsili) told us, 'Abd Allah ibn 'Umar told us, Muhammad ibn Fudayl told us, on the authority of his father, on the authority of Abu Hazim:

Abu Hurayra said, "I was in extremely dire straits. I met 'Umar ibn al-Khattab, and asked him to recite a verse for me from the Book of

---

1. Abu Hurayra (introduced in the previous anecdote) was a companion of the prophet Muhammad and a transmitter of his sayings and deeds. He was a poor man and fond of jokes. When herding goats, his kitten would keep him company, hence the name Abu Hurayra, which means, loosely, "guy with a kitten." Ja'far was a cousin of the Prophet.

God. He went into his house and taught it to me. I walked a short distance away, and then fell on my face from hunger. Suddenly, the Prophet of God was standing by my head.

"'Oh, Abu Hurayra!' he said.

"'I am at your service, Prophet of God,' I replied

"He took me by the hand and raised me up. He saw what was wrong with me. He took me to his camel bag and gave me a bowl of milk, from which I drank.

"'Again, Abu Hurayra,' he said.

"I drank again, and continued drinking until I had filled my belly as full as a goblet. Later I saw 'Umar, and explained to him what had happened.

"'My trouble was resolved by one better suited than you to resolve it,' I said, 'and what's more, I asked you to recite a verse for me that I knew better than you did!'

"'I wish I had taken you in,' said 'Umar, 'more than I wish for a beautiful red camel.'"

99

Abu al-Husayn Muhammad ibn al-Husayn ibn Ahmad al-Ahwazi told us, and he said, I heard al-Hasan ibn 'Abd Allah al-Lughawi say, I heard Abu Bakr ibn Durayd say, I heard Abu Hatim say:

Someone went out to visit a sick man on the edge of Kufa, and Abu Hanifa[2] and Abu Bakr al-Hudhali[3] met him, and he said, "We're visiting So-and-So."

So they followed him to the sick man, visiting him, and Abu Hanifa said to Abu Bakr, "If we sit, he'll bring some lunch."

So when they went in, they began talking, and Abu Bakr recited, "We will surely test you with something of fear and of hunger," to the end of the verse.[4]

The sick man got the hint, so he stretched out and recited, "It is not incumbent upon the weak or the ill" to the end of that verse.[5]

"Get up," said Abu Hanifa. "You're not getting anything good out of him."

2. Abu Hanifa (d. 767) was an Islamic jurist after whom was named the Hanafi school of law.

3. Al-Hudhali was a hadith transmitter.

4. Qur'an 2:155: "And surely We shall try you with something of fear and hunger, and loss of wealth and lives and crops; but give glad tidings to the steadfast" (Pickthal's translation).

5. Qur'an 9:91: "Not unto the weak nor unto the sick nor unto those who can find naught to spend is any fault . . . if they are true to Allah and His messenger. Not unto the good is there any road (of blame). Allah is Forgiving, Merciful" (Pickthal's translation).

100

Abu 'Ali al-Hasan ibn 'Ali ibn 'Abd Allah al-Muqri'
told us, Muhammad ibn Ja'far al-Tamimi al-Kufi
told us, Abu Muhammad al-'Ataki said, I met secretary Ahmad ibn Sa'id al-Ta'i in Damascus, and he
told me:

I was composing poetry, and I wrote these two
lines for Abu Ya'qub. Listen how he answered me:

May God forbid, Abu Ya'qub,
our friendship ever end,
but how shall we be friends
unless your dinners I attend?

And he answered:

You're always at my dinners!
When did I your meal attend?
If things were fair between us,
you would dine alone, my friend!

101

'Ali ibn Abu 'Ali told us, Ibrahim ibn Ahmad ibn
Muhammad al-Muqri' told us, al-Muzaffar ibn Yahya
told us, Abu al-Hasan al-Asadi recited this to us:

Yesterday I might have party-crashed
Did I not fear that you would think me rude.
I bore in mind the guard would be abashed
if I came uninvited for the food.
I felt the other guests would sense a boor,
and God forbid you should be burdened so,
but think me now, who blushes at your door,
an eager virgin, startled at "Hello!"

Those Who Love People to Sponge and Facilitate It

Abu al-Hasan Muhammad ibn 'Abd al-Wahid ibn Muhammad ibn Ja'far told me, Muhammad ibn 'Abd al-Rahim al-Mazini told us, Abu Ahmad al-Hariri told us, Ahmad ibn al-Harith al-Kharraz told us, Abu al-Hasan al-Madini told us:

> Abu Burda said to Ibn al-Sammak, "What do you say, O Abu al-'Abbas, about *jawzinaj*'s light and flaky crust, and the power of its sweetness, drowning in sugar and oiled nuts?"
>
> He replied, "My God, what a description! Positively painful given the absence of what you describe. If the pastry were only here right now, I would savor its presence so much more than your description. But as it is not, please let us do

without more description as we must do without the pastry itself."

104

The judge Abu al-'Ala' Muhammad ibn 'Ali ibn Ya'qub al-Wasiti told us, Muhammad ibn Zayd ibn 'Ali ibn Marwan al-Kufi told us, Muhammad ibn al-Qasim al-Anbari told us, my father related to me, Abu al-Nadr the jurist told me:

> I heard someone tell a story about al-Rashid and a member of his family arguing about *faludhaj* and *lawzinaj*,[1] and which is tastier. Al-Rashid said, "We'll ask Abu al-Harith Jummayn,"[2] and so they went and got him. Al-Rashid said to him,

1. Both *faludhaj* and *lawzinaj* are pastries made of sugar, nuts, and rose water. For recipes, see Charles Perry's translation of a medieval Arabic cookbook, *A Baghdad Cookery Book*, in the chapter on sweets.

2. Abu al-Harith Jummayn was a well-known jester, and Harun al-Rashid (d. 809) was the fifth and most famous of the Abbasid caliphs. His was a life particularly prone to "dramatic enhancement," and Tayeb al-Hibri writes that authors were fond of portraying the idealized caliph as "accessible to every fortune-seeking poet and jester between the Nile and the Oxus" (*Reinterpreting Islamic Historiography*, 28).

"Hey, Abu al-Harith, what do you think about *faludhaj* and *lawzinaj*—which is tastier?"

"O Commander of the Faithful," he answered, "I cannot pronounce upon them in absentia." So al-Rashid said, "Somebody go get him some," and Abu al-Harith set to eating a great deal of *faludhaj*, and then a great deal of *lawzinaj*, until al-Rashid said to him, "Now tell us which is tastier. Choose one of the two."

"O Commander of the Faithful," said Abu al-Harith, "whenever I attempt to pass a verdict, the other begs me to consider its case once more . . ."

105

Abu al-Qasim al-Azhari told me, Muhammad ibn Sulayman ibn al-Khidr told us, Abu Ishaq Ibrahim ibn Ja'far al-Tustari told us, Ahmad ibn al-Hasan al-Basri told us, Ahmad ibn al-Isbahani told us, Abu Bakr ibn 'Abd Allah al-Isbahani said, al-Hasan ibn al-Sabah al-Nasa'i said:

I paid Ja'far ibn Muhammad a visit, and he asked me, "What do you think about sweets?"

"I will not judge an absentee," I told him.

So he called for a four-legged polished conical bowl filled with *lawzinaj* and *ma'mul* of a red rose water, almonds stripped of their shells, white sugar, all coiled in a pale honey, such that if you broke the *lawzinaj*, you could hear it creak like an Indian shoe, and when you put it in your mouth, it would crackle like iron just out of the bellows.

And I said, "And your God is one God," and Ja'far fed me one.[3]

Then I said, "He sent to them two."[4]

So he fed me a second. Then I said, "He fortified us with a third."[5]

So he fed me a third. Then I said, "Then take four birds."[6]

---

3. All of these quotes are fragments of Qur'anic verses. Although some found such playful misuses of the holy text objectionable, they were fairly widespread. Geert Jan van Gelder, "Forbidden Firebrands: Frivolous *Iqtibas* (Quotations from the Qur'an) According to Medieval Arab Critics," 3–14. This quote is from 2:163.

4. Qur'an 36:14.

5. Qur'an 36:14.

6. Qur'an 2:260, as translated by Abdullah Yusuf Ali: "When Abraham said: 'Show me, Lord, how You will raise the dead,' He replied: 'Have you no faith?' He said 'Yes, but just to reassure my heart.' Allah said, 'Take four birds, draw them to you, and cut their bodies to pieces. Scatter them over the mountain-tops, then call them back. They will come swiftly to you. Know that Allah is Mighty, Wise.'"

So he fed me a fourth. Then I said, "There is no secret conference of three, but He is their fourth, nor of five . . ."[7]

So he fed me a fifth. Then I said, "Say they were five, the dog being the sixth . . ."[8]

So he fed me a sixth. Then I said, "Seven heavens one above another."[9]

So he fed me a seventh. Then I said, "Eight pairs . . ."[10]

So he fed me an eighth. Then I said, "Nine men . . ."[11]

So he fed me a ninth. Then I said, "Ten in all . . ."[12]

7. Qur'an 58:7.

8. Qur'an 18:22, which says (as translated by Yusuf Ali): "(Some) say they were three, the dog being the fourth among them; (others) say they were five, the dog being the sixth,— doubtfully guessing at the unknown; (yet others) say they were seven, the dog being the eighth. Say thou: 'My Lord knoweth best their number; it is but few that know their (real case). Enter not, therefore, into controversies concerning them, except on a matter that is clear, nor consult any of them about (the affair of) the Sleepers.'"

9. Qur'an 67:3, as translated by Yusuf Ali.

10. Qur'an 6:143, which says (as translated by Pickthall): "Eight pairs: Of the sheep twain, and of the goats twain." The Sura contains laws concerning cattle.

11. Qur'an 27:48, as translated by Yusuf Ali.

12. Qur'an 2:196.

So he fed me a tenth. Then I said, "I saw eleven stars . . ."[13]

So he fed me an eleventh. Then I said, "Surely, the number of months with Allah is twelve months in Allah's ordinance."[14]

So he fed me a twelfth, and I said, "If there be of you twenty steadfast . . ."[15]

And he hurled the bowl at me and said, "So eat, you bastard," and I replied, "By God, if you hadn't thrown this bowl at me, I would have said, "And we sent him to a hundred thousand or more!"[16]

13. Qur'an 12:4, referring to Joseph's prophetic dream in which he sees eleven stars and the sun and the moon bowing before him.
14. Qur'an 9:36.
15. Qur'an 8:65.
16. Qur'an 37:147.

Anecdotes about Party-Crashers Who Exert Themselves in Party-Crashing and Make It a Trade and Occupation

106

Abu ʿAbd Allah al-Husayn ibn Muhammad ibn al-Hasan, brother of al-Khallal told me, Ibrahim ibn ʿAbd Allah ibn Ibrahim al-Shatti in Jurjan told me, Abu ʿAli Shuʿba told us:

> The party-crashing chieftains in Basra were very dashing, sporting blue wraps in the summertime. One of these chieftains, called "Abu Malik al-Halik," was walking down Quraysh Lane on a Saturday evening, when he ran into Abu ʿAbd Allah Muhammad ibn Ibrahim ibn Ishaq. Muhammad ibn Ibrahim was sitting by the door and had just swept the sidewalk, because he was

Takeout

marrying the daughter of Husayn ibn Bishr al-
Sabuni that Sunday. So Abu Malik said, "Hello"
and "Congratulations," and then he said, "I heard
that you're going to have a big feast tomorrow. If
it's okay, I'm going to come to your house, eat at
the banquet, and slip some food out for the kids."

"Okay," said Muhammad ibn Ibrahim.

So the next day Abu Malik showed up, walked
in on the banquet, ate his fill, and brought some
food back for the kids too.

107

I read in a book of al-Hasan ibn Abi Ya'qub al-Isbahani's, Muhammad ibn 'Abd Allah ibn Asid al-Madini

86

told us, Muhammad ibn Zakariyya al-Ghalabi told us, Muhammad ibn Khalid ibn 'Amr said:

> A group of party-crashers gathered to crash a banquet, and their leader said, "Oh, God, let not the gatekeepers push us from the front, nor shove us from the back, nor knock us about the head, but grant to us his mercy and his goodwill, and facilitate for us the obtaining of his permission." And when they entered, they were received by the cook, and the leader called him "Blessed first and best one to greet us, bringing plenty and banishing lack." And when they sat at the table, he said to it, "May God make you blessed like Moses's staff, Abraham's table, Jesus's supper."
>
> Then he said to his friends, "Open your mouths and straighten your gullets, roll up your sleeves and loosen your belts, and chew not with the jaw of the ailing, nor the stomach of dyspepsia, and yet recall that days may soon turn black, and all go awry."[1]

1. The entire anecdote parodies religious language. The final instructions, for example, mimic the traditional instructions, as established by Muhammad, given to Muslims before prayer. Van Gelder writes that prayers such as these are "at the same time pious and parodic" (*Of Dishes and Discourse*, 91).

108

Abu al-Hasan 'Ali ibn al-Husayn ibn Muhammad ibn Ibrahim told us, 'Ali ibn al-Hasan al-Razi told us, al-Husayn ibn al-Qasim al-Kawkabi told us, Ibn Sadaqa related to me:

> Once somebody asked a party-crasher how well he knew the Book of God, and the party-crasher responded, "I'm one of the most knowledgeable people there is on the subject." So someone said, "What does, 'Ask the town that we were in' mean?" He said, "It means, 'Ask the people *in* the town.'" And someone asked him if he had proof for that, and the party-crasher said, "It's like when you say 'I ate the whole table,' which just means, 'I ate what was on the table.'"[2]

109

Ahmad ibn Abi Ja'far al-Qati'i told us, 'Ali ibn al-Hasan ibn al-Mutaraffiq al-Tarsusi told us, I heard 'Abd Allah ibn 'Adi say, I heard 'Isma ibn Kamal say:

2. They are discussing a passage from the Sura 12, Yusuf, verse 82 in the Qur'an.

I heard Abu 'Amr the party-crasher say, "I heard my teacher say about 'Thereafter they return only to Hell'[3] (a saying of God Almighty), 'It has something to do with food.'"

110

This interpretation is similar to that which was told to me by Abu Nu'aym Ahmad ibn 'Abd Allah al-Hafiz, that he heard Abu Bakr ibn al-Muqri' interpret Khidr's advice to Moses, "Walk not when there is no need," to mean, "Don't walk somewhere you're not going to chew something."

111

Muhammad ibn 'Ali ibn al-Hasan al-Jallab told me:

A party-crasher had this verse inscribed on his signet ring: "Will ye not eat?"[4]

3. Qur'an 37:68.
4. Qur'an 37:91, as translated by Pickthall. In this verse Abraham addresses false idols who cannot eat the food offerings of their worshipers. It was traditional to inscribe Qur'an verses on signet rings, though this seems a frivolous choice.

112

And he said, "A party-crasher said, 'The three best places are the head shop, the grilled meat shop, and the pastry shop.'"

113

I read under al-Hasan ibn Abu al-Qasim on the authority of al-Faraj 'Ali ibn al-Husayn al-Isbahani, al-'Abbas ibn 'Ali al-Suli told me:

> "Why are you so pale?" somebody asked a party-crasher.
>
> "We were between courses, and I was afraid that the food had run out!" he said.

114

Abu Muslim Ahmad ibn Muhammad ibn 'Abd al-Rahman ibn Bundar al-Qadi related to us, I read this in a book written by my father:

> Someone said to a party-crasher, "Do you love Abu Bakr and 'Umar?"[5]

5. Abu Bakr and 'Umar were the first two successors of the prophet Muhammad.

"Food has left no place in my heart for loving anyone," he replied.

115

I heard someone say, on the authority of a party-crasher:

AIf you are sitting at a table, don't talk while you are eating. If someone addresses you in such a way that you must respond, answer only "*na'm*" (yes), for conversation distracts from eating, but saying "*na'm*" assists in chewing.

116

Al-Husayn ibn Muhammad al-Rafiqi told us in his book, 'Ali ibn Muhammad ibn al-Sari told us, Ahmad ibn al-Hasan al-Muqri' said:

'Abbas the sponger was asked, "What would you most like to have happen to you unexpectedly?"
"I'd like to be invited somewhere nearby on a rainy day," he answered.[6]

6. Not only does this proposition sound especially cozy, but rain was a common metaphor for openhanded generosity, the hope of all party-crashers.

117

Muhammad ibn 'Ali al-Jallab related to me:

A party-crasher went out on a trip with a group of people. They'd decided that each would contribute something to the fare. "I came with such and such," they each said, one by one. But when they got to the party-crasher, he simply said, "I came," and fell silent.

"What did you come with?" they asked him.

"God's curse on my head!" he said.

They all laughed at that, and excused him from contributing to the fare. They took him along on their trip.

118

Al-Husayn ibn Muhammad al-Rafiqi informed us, Ibn Muhammad ibn al-Sari told us, Ahmad ibn al-Hasan Hasan al-Muqri' told us, al-Harith ibn Abi Usama told us, I hear al-Mada'ini say:

A party-crasher walked into a wedding feast, and when they brought out the table and presented the roast, he looked at it and said, "God may judge between the two of us, for it's on your account that I'm here at all!"

119

Ahmad ibn al-Husayn said, I heard Muhammad ibn
Yahya al-Kisa'i say:

> A party-crasher passed by a group who had decided
> to dedicate their day to drinking, and were sitting
> in a parlor for that purpose. He greeted them and
> said to himself, "Should I go in?"
> He went in.

Lazy

"Young men," he said to them, "what are you sitting around for?"

"We sent someone to get us some meat," they said.

When the meat arrived, the cook asked them, "What would you like to be cooked?"

"Juniper kabab," the party-crasher answered.

When he had eaten, he reclined and crossed his legs.

"Whose house is this?" he wondered.

Then he answered himself, thinking, "It's yours, man, until someone says otherwise."

120

'Ali ibn al-Muhassin ibn 'Ali al-Qadi related to me on the authority of his father:

A party-crasher took up with a man while traveling. One day the man said to him, "Go and buy some meat for us."

"No, by God, I don't have the means," said the party-crasher.

So the man went and bought the meat. Then he said, "Get up and cook it."

"I'm no good at cooking," said the party-crasher.

So the man cooked the meat. Then he said, "Get up and sop the bread," and the party-crasher replied, "By God, I feel exhausted."

So the man sopped the bread. Then he said, "Get up and ladle the stew."

"I'm afraid I'll spill it on my robe," said the party-crasher, so the man ladled the stew.

"Get up and eat," he said.

"By God," said the party-crasher, "I've been feeling bad for refusing you so many times," and he came forward and ate.

121

Ahmad ibn Abi Ja'far told us, 'Ali ibn al-Hasan ibn al-Mutaraffiq al-Tarsusi in Egypt told us, I heard 'Abd Allah ibn 'Adi say, I heard Muhammad ibn 'Ubayd Allah say, I heard al-Jahiz say:

I asked Abu Sa'id the party-crasher, "How much is four plus four?"

"Two loaves of bread and one piece of meat," he replied.

122

Abu al-Hasan 'Ali ibn Ayub al-Qummi told me, Abu 'Ubayd Allah Muhammad 'Imran al-Marzubani told us, 'Abd Allah ibn Ja'far related to me, Abu al-'Abbas al-Mubarrad told us:

Someone asked a party-crasher, "What is two times two?"

"Four loaves of bread," he replied.

And another time he said, "I waited the amount of time it takes someone to eat a loaf of bread."

123

Abu Ya'la Ahmad ibn 'Abd al-Wahid al-Wakil told us, Isma'il ibn Sa'id ibn Isma'il al-Mu'addal told me, al-Husayn ibn al-Qasim al-Kawkabi told us, al-Haddadi told us, Abu Hiffan said:

Someone asked a party-crasher, "What's four times four?"

"Sixteen loaves of bread," he said.

And Abu Hiffan said:

"Once a man crashed another man's party.

"'Who are you?' the host asked him.

"'I'm the one who saved you the trouble of sending an invitation!' he replied."

And Abu Hiffan recited:

Whether the rest came early or late,
I arrive when the cook's a-ladling.

124

I read under al-Hasan ibn Abi al-Qasim on the authority of Abu al-Faraj 'Ali ibn al-Husayn al-Isbahani, Abu 'Abd Allah Muhammad ibn Ahmad al-Katib told me, Ja'far ibn Abi al-Fadl the poet told us, my father told me:

> Once a party-crasher walked in the house of a man who had invited a gathering of people.
>
> "Hey, you!" the man said. "Did I say you could come?"
>
> "Did you say I *couldn't* come?" the party-crasher replied.

125

Muhammad al-Hasan 'Ubayd Allah al-Bazzaz related to me:

> A party-crasher walked into a gathering, and they said to him, "Nobody invited you!"
>
> "But if you didn't invite me *and* I didn't come," he replied, "think how lonely that would be!"
>
> Everybody laughed at that, and they let him stay.

127

Muhammad ibn 'Ali ibn al-Hasan al-Jallab related to us:

> A man was invited to a party, and a party-crasher followed him there. The host realized what had happened and wanted to let the party-crasher know that he realized it, so he greeted them, saying, "I don't know who to thank more—you who took the trouble to answer my invitation, or you who took the trouble without an invitation to answer!"

Accounts of the Ones That the Guards Would Refuse, but Who Outwit the Guards with a Lie or a Ruse

128

Al-Husayn ibn Muhammad ibn Ja'far al-Rafiqi informed us, 'Ali ibn Muhammad ibn al-Sari al-Hamadhani told us, Ahmad ibn al-Hasan al-Muqri' said:

Bunan passed by a wedding and wanted to get in, but couldn't. So he went to the grocer and put his ring down in exchange for ten cups of chewable honey.

Then he returned to the gate of the wedding and said, "Hey, gatekeeper! Open up!" And the gatekeeper said, "Who are you?"

"I see that you don't recognize me!" Bunan replied. "I'm the guy who was supposed to get the honey cups," so the gatekeeper opened the gate and Bunan went in. He ate and drank with the crowd, and when he'd had enough, he took the honey cups again and called to the gatekeeper, "Open up! They want plain honey, so I've got to return these cups." He went out and returned them to the grocer, and got his ring back.

129

And he said:

Bunan went to a banquet only to have the door shut in his face, so he borrowed a ladder, leaned it against the man's wall, and climbed up. Then he began watching the man's daughters from above. "Hey, you!" the man called. "Do you not fear God? You're looking at my daughters!"

"O Sheikh!" Bunan replied. "Well dost thou know we have no need of thy daughters: indeed, thou knowest quite well what we want!"[1]

Then the man laughed and said, "Come down and eat, then."

1. The Qur'anic verse that Bunan quotes is 11:79, Hud, in which the lusty crowds of Sodom respond to Lot, who has attempted to appease them with his daughters. These crowds, unlike the party-crasher, were not after food.

"Hey!" said Bunan. "Don't think ill of your elders next time, and ask God to forgive you for what just happened."

130

There was a tale of this sort told about Ash'ab ibn Jubayr, a master of wit in Medina:

'Ali ibn Abi 'Ali told us, Isma'il ibn Sa'id al-Mu'addal told us, Abu Bakr ibn al-Anbari said, Mus'ab al-Zubayri said that:

Salim ibn 'Abd Allah was out for a picnic with all of his women in one of the parks of the city. Ash'ab caught wind of this and thought he would drop by for some party-crashing. He found the park gate locked and began to scale the wall, when Salim said, "Damn it, Ash'ab! My daughters and my lady are with me!" Ash'ab responded, "Well dost thou know we have no need of thy daughters: indeed, thou knowest quite well what we want!"

So Salim gave him some food—some to eat and some to take home.

131

Muhammad ibn 'Ali al-Jallab related to me:

A party-crasher came to a wedding and was denied entry. He happened to know that the bride's brother was absent, so he left and got a piece of paper. He folded it up like a letter, and he sealed it (although there was nothing inside), and he addressed it "From the brother to the bride." He went back.

"I have a note from the bride's brother for her," he said.

He received permission to go in and present the letter.

"We've never seen an address like this before," everybody said. "It has no name on it!"

"What's even stranger than that," said the party-crasher, "is that there's nothing inside—not one letter! That's because he was in a big hurry when he wrote it."

Everybody laughed. They knew it was a trick to get in, and they let him get away with it.

132

Muhammad ibn ʿAli said to me:

There was a party-crasher named Waylon, and somebody asked him, "What do you do if they won't let you into a wedding?"

Waylon

He said, "I start wailin' by the door until people get sick of it and invite me in."[2]

133

Muhammad ibn 'Ali 'Ubayd Allah al-Karkhi related to me:

2. The party-crasher's name is actually "Nuh" (Noah), which sounds like the verb *to mourn* or *to wail*.

A party-crasher couldn't get into a wedding, so he took one of his shoes and hid it in his sleeve and hung the other from his arm, and then he got a toothpick and borrowed a dirty dish from the perfumer. He dipped the toothpick in the dish and stuck it in his teeth, and went running back to the gatekeeper as if in a big hurry. He said to him, "I ate with the first table at the banquet because I had to leave early for work, and in my hurry I took one of my shoes and forgot the other. Could you please bring it out to me?" The gatekeeper said, "I'm too busy. Go in and get it yourself." So the party-crasher went in and ate, and then he left again.

134

Some of the storytellers mentioned that Abu al-'Abbas al-Mubarrad recited this poem of al-Hamduni's about a party-crasher:

> I see you will show up at every wedding—
>   inevitable as the Will of God,
> and if you find the doorman rough and ready,
> and if you find the limen tough and hard,
> a toothpick in your teeth, thus you address
>   them,
> "I left my sandal with you, if you please,"

and then approach the table and its banquet,
to tuck the choicest bits inside your sleeve!
You pick the dishes of the richest flavor,
and never fail to save some for your wife.
You are so very skilled, you party-crasher!
You've never missed a party in your life!

135

Abu Muhammad al-Hasan ibn 'Isa ibn al-Muqtadir
Billah told us, Abu al-'Abbas Ahmad ibn Mansur al-
Yashkuri told us, Ibn al-Anbari told us, my father
related to me, Ahmad ibn 'Ubayd told us on the
authority of Abu 'Ubayda, and he said:

We were visiting a Banu Makhzum man, who
was staying in the vicinity of the Banu Tamim,
and Dukayn al-Rajiz showed up and said to the
gatekeeper, "I am fainting for some hot food! Let
me in!"

The gatekeeper refused to let him in, so
Dukayn stood by some nearby shops where some
people had come out, and started to say,

People gathered and said "a wedding!"
With five big bowls and five little guests
and Zalajlajas moving around,
with darting eyes, and sighing chests . . .

The gatekeeper said to him, "Who are you, god-damn you?!" He said, "I'm Dukayn al-Rajiz!"[3] so he let him in.

Abu Bakr ibn al-Anbari said, the interpretation of this story was told to me by my father, who said that Ahmad ibn 'Ubayd said "fainting for" means "burning with desire for, when the heart is on fire with longing for something." And the Zalajlajas are women moving and coming and going and never stopping in one place.

136

Al-Husayn ibn Muhammad al-Rafiqi informed us, 'Ali ibn Muhammad ibn al-Sari Ahmad ibn al-Hasan al-Muqri' told us, Muhammad ibn Ahmad al-Muqri' told us, saying:

A party-crasher threw a banquet, and two party-crashers showed up. He recognized them, and sent them up to a room. He fed whom he wanted, and then brought the party-crashers back down and said, "Happy trails!" and sent them on their way without eating a thing.

3. Dukayn al-Rajiz was a poet from the eighth century.

Happy Trails

137

There was a witty story to this effect told about Abu Saʻid ibn Darraj, the party-crasher:

Abu Bakr Ahmad ibn ʻAli al-Muqriʼ al-Wasiti told me, ʻUbayd Allah ibn Muhammad ibn Ahmad al-Bazzaz told us, Jaʻfar ibn Muhammad ibn al-Qasim told us, Abu al-ʻAbbas al-Tusi told us, Ibn

Abu Sa'd told us, Muhammad ibn 'Amr told us, Abu 'Ali al-Qurashi told me that:

> Ibn Darraj, the party-crasher, who was of the Harran household, came to Baghdad, and he passed by the gate of a house that was holding a banquet, so he went in. It happened that the owner of the house had erected a ladder and was instructing people he did not recognize to "go up, my friend."
>
> As Ibn Darraj related, "I climbed up to a room, and there I found thirteen other party-crashers. The host then took the ladder away, and a table was set on the level below. My companions were bewildered. 'Nothing like this has ever happened to us before,' they said.
>
> "'Young gentlemen,' I said to them [Ibn Darraj continued], 'what is your trade?'
>
> "'The crashing of parties,' they replied.
>
> "'And what do you have to say about the situation we are in?' I asked.
>
> "'We don't have a solution,' they said.
>
> "'If I solve this for you so that you get to eat and to go back down,' I said, 'will you acknowledge me as your teacher in party-crashing?'
>
> "'Who are you, by God?' they asked.
>
> "'I am Ibn Darraj,' I told them.
>
> "'We already acknowledge you, even before you solve this problem for us,' they said.

"So I located the owner of the house [Ibn Darraj continued], and carefully regarded him and the people eating.

"'Owner of the house!' I called.

"'What's the problem?' he asked.

"'Which would you prefer?' I said. 'You can bring us up a big table so that we can eat and come down afterward, or I'll throw myself down on my head and be carried out of your house killed, and this party will turn into a funeral!' and I began to hike up my trousers as though I were about to run and hurl myself down.

"Then the owner of the house said, 'Calm down, damn you, don't do it!' and he quickly brought the things. 'This guy is crazy,' he said, and they lifted the table up to us. We ate and came down."

Ibn Darraj was a party-crasher of old, and there are many well-known stories about him.

138

Ahmad ibn 'Ali ibn al-Husayn al-Muhtasib told me, 'Ubayd Allah ibn Muhammad al-Muqri' told us, Ja'far ibn Muhammad al-Tusi told us, Ibn Abi Sa'd told us, Muhammad ibn 'Amr related to us, Abu 'Ali al-Qurayshi related to us:

I heard 'Isa ibn Muhammad ibn Abi Khalid ask Ibn Darraj, whose head was narrow, "Why is your head so narrow?"

"From doing battle with gates," he said, by which he meant that his head had been pressed between a wall and a gate.

139

Al-Husayn ibn Muhammad al-Rafiqi informed us, 'Ali ibn Muhammad ibn al-Sari Ahmad ibn al-Hasan al-Muqri' told us, Abu 'Abd Allah ibn al-Jahm related to us, Yahya al-Farra' told us:

I hired Ibn Darraj, the party-crasher, to dictate thirty jokes and sayings to me for a dirham, but when he recited a tired joke, I wouldn't credit it to his account.

"If you wanted the good jokes," he said, "it's *ten* for a dirham!"

Mention of the Party-Crashers' Conversations, Advice, and Poetry

140

Abu Muslim Ahmad ibn Muhammad ibn 'Abd al-Rahman ibn Bundar al-Qadi in Qasan related to me, I read in a book written in my father's hand:

A party-crasher was blamed for his party-crashing, and he said, "What was food made for except to be eaten? What was the table laid for except to be enjoyed? Households aren't maintained except to be entered. I've never given a gift hoping for an invitation, and I don't dislike being rude to someone who seems stingy with my food. So I burst into a party, and I take command of the social situation, and I smile at anyone I see frowning, and eat my fill in spite of him, and

after I've gorged myself I eat again just to give
him a pain. And I don't spend one dirham or
wear out my servant. In regards to all this, I say:

Each day I rove the courtyard with the fly
who buzzes 'round the scent of roasted meat
and if there's but a stirring or a sigh
of dinner guests, or catered meet-and-greet,
I never fear to jeer and push on by
the guard, and circle like an eagle free,
I sneer at someone giving me the eye,
unburdened of the least anxiety
about the butcher or the veggie guy . . . [1]

141

It was told on the authority of Ibn Da'b that these
verses are from Abu al-'Araqib al-Madani, the party-
crasher, and they begin:

Tell the party-crashers far and wide,
I am your leader, young and elderly!

And at the end he mentioned more lines in addi-
tion to what we've quoted, with a few variations
of expression:

[1]. Another version of this poem is given below in anecdote 152.

And I don't need approval high or low,
You don't see me run from man or dog,
The people fear that I will tear their clothes . . .

142

Abu al-Qasim al-Azhari related to us, Ahmad ibn
Ibrahim ibn Shadhan told us, Ahmad ibn Mas'ud
ibn 'Amr told us, Ibrahim ibn 'Abd al-Salam told
us, Bishr ibn Hayyan told us, Sulayman al-Minqari
told us:

I was at one of my friend's parties, and there was
a party-crasher in the crowd. One of the other
guests began to stare at him suspiciously.

"Hey, young man," said the party-crasher,
"praise God, didn't you hear that the Prophet,
peace and prayers upon him, forbid a man to
stare at someone who is eating?"

The man turned to me and said, "Did you
know that?"

"No, by God!" I answered. I left the party.
I've been asking around about it ever since.[2]

2. Although Sulayman al-Minqari was unable to find the
party-crasher's hadith, al-Khatib al-Baghdadi evidently man-
aged to do so and provides it below.

143

Abu ʿAmir al-ʿUqdi related to us, Sufyan ibn Salama told us, al-Khallal, brother of Ibn Salama and father of ʿUmar said on the authority of ʿAbd Allah ibn Abi Bakr ibn Muhammad ibn ʿAmr ibn Hazm, on the authority of his father, that:

> The Prophet, peace and prayers upon him, forbade a man to stare at a companion while he is eating.

145

The judge Abu al-ʿAla' Muhammad ibn ʿAli ibn Yaʿqub al-Wasiti told us, Abu al-Hasan ʿAli ibn Ahmad ibn al-Hasan al-Hafiz told us, Abu al-Husayn Muhammad ibn ʿUthman ibn Abu al-ʿAs al-Thaqafi in Basra told us, Bakr ibn Ahmad ibn Sakhit al-Qazzaz al-Farisi told us, Nasr ibn ʿAli Abu ʿAmr al-Jahdami related to us:[3]

3. This is the anecdote that first drew al-Khatib al-Baghdadi's interest to the subject of party-crashing, possibly because it involves a discussion of hadith and al-Khatib al-Baghdadi was a hadith scholar. See the introduction for his first mention of the tale.

I had a neighbor who was a party-crasher, and he was one of the best-looking and best-spoken people, and the best perfumed and most finely dressed as well. It was his custom to follow me when I was invited to a gathering, and people did honors to him on my account because they assumed that he was my friend.

So it came to happen that Ja'far ibn al-Qasim al-Hashimi, prince of Basra, wanted to celebrate the circumcision of one of his sons, and I said to myself, "I'm probably going to get an invitation from the prince, and this man is probably going to follow me again. By God, if he follows me this time, I'm really going to teach him a lesson!"

And I was like that right up until the arrival of the messenger with the invitation.

No sooner had I put on my robe and stepped out the door but I saw the party-crasher waiting for me by the gate of his house, ready to go. I set off, and he followed me. After we entered the prince's house, we sat for a while, and then the food was called out and tables were brought, and everybody was pressed around the tables because there were so many people.

I proceeded to one of these tables with the party-crasher on my heels, but just as he reached out his hand and began to grab the food, I said, "Durust ibn Ziyad told us on the authority of Aban ibn Tariq on the authority of Nafi' on

115

the authority of ibn 'Umar, 'The messenger of God, prayers and peace upon him, said, "He who enters a gathering to which he was not invited and eats their food enters as a thief and leaves as a looter."'"

When he heard that he said, "By God, I thumb my nose at you, Abu 'Amr! And there's not one man among this crowd but thinks that you just insinuated something about him! Aren't you ashamed to talk like that at the very table of he who feeds the people, and to play the miser with food that isn't even yours? And aren't you ashamed to cite the unreliable hadith transmitter Durust ibn Ziyad on the authority of Aban ibn Tariq, who is unreliable as well? And yet on his authority you pass judgments that go against the Prophet himself—for the thief's punishment is cutting of the hands, and the looters' is as the imam sees fit—but according to this hadith related to us by Abu 'Asim al-Nabil, on the authority of Ibn Jurayj, on the authority of Abu al-Zubayr, on the authority of Jabir, 'The messenger of God, prayers and peace upon him, said, "Food for one is enough for two, and food for two is enough for four, and food for four is enough for eight."' And this is a sound text with a sound chain of transmission!"

"I was dumbfounded," said Nasr ibn 'Ali, "and no reply came to my mind. When we left the party, he crossed to the other side of the

116

street after he had been walking behind me, and
I heard him say:

He who thinks to begin a war
and suffer no harm, think again!

146

Al-Husayn ibn Muhammad al-Rafiqi informed us,
'Ali ibn Muhammad ibn al-Sari told us, Ahmad ibn
al-Hasan al-Muqri' told us:

One day Bunan got scolded, and I overheard.

"Damn you, Bunan!" someone said to him.
"What's all this you're getting into, getting fed!
Seek God's forgiveness for the business that
you're in!"

"May I be your ransom," Bunan replied.
"Who denies himself white and yellow semolina,
suckling kid, or dense *faludhaj*? No, by God, the
intelligent never refuse them, nor does a free
man abstain!"

147

And he said:

Bunan had eaten and eaten well, and someone
said to him, "Slow down! You'll kill yourself!"

"If it is time to die," Bunan replied, "I want to go well fed and well watered, not parched and hungry."

150

Al-Husayn ibn Muhammad al-Rafiqi informed us, 'Ali ibn Muhammad ibn al-Sari said, Ahmad ibn al-Hasan al-Muqri' said:

A man said to Bunan, "Counsel me!"

"Don't fraternize," he replied, "but if you can't avoid it, pick someone who won't pester you. Don't go for greens, gorge on chicken skin, stuff yourself with goat kidneys, gulp bird gizzards, snatch fish innards, or concern yourself with the eyeballs if a head is served. And pay no attention to skinny poultry. Think of naught but what is on your plate, nor glance upon the plates of the others. And if the roast goat when passed to you has little meat left on it, pity not the weakness of the aged guests, nor the greed of the young. Eat, and don't bother yourself with the host's family, and don't waste time inquiring after their health.

151

Abu Talib Muhammad ibn 'Abd Allah ibn al-Hasan al-Kirmani told us, I heard Abu al-Faraj Muhammad ibn 'Ubayd Allah al-Shirazi mentioned that:

A party-crasher was laid up with an illness, and his slave boy came to him for counsel.

The party-crasher said, "May God graciously bestow bodily health upon you, and a lot of food, and a lengthy appetite, and a strong stomach. May he grant you teeth that grind and a stomach that digests, as well as holding capacity, even temperament, security, and vigor . . .

"If you are seated at the table a long way from the water and you choke on a piece of food, put your right hand above your head and shake it like you're adjusting your sleeve, and, God permitting, the food will go down.

"If your place at the table is too small, say to whoever's sitting beside you, 'Excuse me, Mr. So-and-So. Perhaps I'm crowding you a little?' and he'll move back a bit and say, 'No, praise God, I've got plenty of room,' thus giving you more space.

"If a dish comes your way at the table, don't pass it by, thinking, 'Maybe something better will come along.'"

"Go on!" said the slave boy.

He said, "If there's only a little bit of bread, eat the crusts. If there's a lot, eat only the middle.

"Don't drink a lot of water while eating, because it prevents you from eating as much, and that is the pinnacle of stupidity."

"Go on," said the slave boy.

"Eat each dish," he said, "as though you've never seen anything like it before, and hoard it as though it's exceedingly rare."

"Go on," said the slave boy.

"If," he said, "you find food, consider it a provision for your journey to God.

"Don't eat flat bread folded, or it will trouble you. Eat it mashed, so you can get your teeth around it, and it's easier to chew.

"If you go to a wedding that's very crowded, pass it by. Also if the gatekeeper is burly and insolent, pass him by, lest he deal with you roughly.

"Let your comments lie somewhere between advice and braggadocio. For example, I once went to a banquet and there was an oaf there— a chef—preoccupied with something he was doing. I went over and saw that he had made a meat pastry and was setting it in the center of the table, where there was an empty spot in case a guest brought a dish.

"'Did our host give you permission to do that?' I asked him.

He had not met me and didn't know who I was, so he responded, 'Hello, sir! I did not know that I needed permission to do this.'

"'Are you drunk?!' I asked him. 'Do you want to impose more food on these people than they can eat and spoil their meal? Truly, you are the dumbest of the dumb! The host of the banquet is going to be very displeased. I would never hide what you've done from him, except that I'm afraid of his disapproval . . .'

"The chef said, 'Save me from his wrath, and I'll split my earnings with you!'

"'I'll do it,' I said.

"I stuck to my promise and ate everything that I wanted, commanding and rejecting dishes as I pleased. The chef was thinking that I had a close relationship to the host, or maybe was related to one of the women.

"Afterward, I vowed secrecy with the chef and took half of his earnings.

"He later found out who I really was, but he forgave me."

152

I read under al-Hasan ibn Abi al-Qasim on the authority of Abu al-Faraj 'Ali ibn al-Husayn al-Isbahani, Ja'far ibn Qudama related to me, Abu Hiffan told me:

A party-crasher went to a gathering, and the owner of the house asked him, "And who might you be, may God forgive you?"

The party-crasher replied, "I'm the guy who says:

Each day I haunt your courtyard with the fly
who buzzes 'round the scent of roasted meat,

and if there's but a stirring or a sigh
of dinner guests, or catered meet-and-greet,
then I, the shameless portal-crasher, I,
circling 'round, just like the eagle free,
pass the scowling guardsman proudly by
unburdened of the least anxiety
about the butcher or the veggie guy.
What pain I wouldn't suffer for a sweet!
Ah, what I wouldn't go through for a pie!"

153

Muhammad ibn al-Hasan ibn 'Ubayd Allah al-Bazzaz recited this poem of Muslimi's for me:

When I see people stingy with their wealth
without a smile of kindness to their name,
or pity for the hungry and the poor,
I play a little party-crashing game,
I leave the trappings of my wealth at home
then loiter at the miser's proud buffet
as if in my own family's dining room.
. . . There are two types of men, I always say:
those who're given food because they're noble,
those who aren't, and eat it anyway.

154

He also recited another one:

We are the people, who, when treated rough,
always cling more tightly to the roughest.
Nor do we mind much if the party's host
sent us an invite or if he rebuffed us.

155

The judge Abu al-Qasim 'Ali ibn al-Muhassin al-
Tanukhi recited this poem by a party-crasher to us:

My praise to party-crashing!
My longtime full support!
How often did I profit
from the party-crashing sport!
Eating life like bread,
all by the party-crasher's art,
and finding in its company
elixirs for the heart!
Though unknown at the party,
I could gossip with the best.
No need to curry boors and fools
when party-crashing blessed!
I'd march right to the banquet
and I didn't care to wait
for invitation messengers
a-knocking at my gate . . .
but tell me where they gather now
at meager spreads or fair?
For I forgot the signs that say

a party's brewing here,
and I forgot that dearest art
of my more youthful years . . .

156

Abu Ya'la Yahya ibn al-Hasan al-Muqri' recited one
of their poems to me:

> We are the people who answer an invite,
> but if we're forgotten, we answer Tatfil.[4]
> We say, "Well, perhaps we were out of the house,
> when the invite came 'round calling us to the
>   meal."
> And we turn our speech to the sweetest of deeds
> like lovers arriving will show how they feel.

157

Muhammad ibn 'Ali ibn 'Ubayd Allah al-Karkhi
told me this poem by somebody else:

> We are the slaves of the stomach, we eat
> what calls to it, even unto Paradise.
> We eat what comes to us. Especially we eat
> what comes to us without a price.

4. *Tatfil* means "party-crashing."

158

Ibrahim ibn Makhlad told us, Ahmad ibn Kamil al-Qadi recited to us, Ahmad ibn Yahya recited this poem by a party-crasher to us:

> We came across the worst kind of deal,
> a low-life who farts when he stands.
> He slammed the door in our faces and then
> appointed a door-keeping man.

159

Abu Ya'la Ahmad ibn 'Abd al-Wahid al-Wakil told us, Isma'il ibn Sa'id al-Mu'addal told us, al-Husayn ibn al-Qasim al-Kawkabi told us, Ibn Abi Tahir told us, Hammad ibn Ishaq informed us on the authority of his father:

> An Arab Bedouin said he approached a man's banquet seeking payment of a debt, and got pushed back, so he said, "*We came across the worst kind of deal*," and recited the rest of the lines.

160

Muhammad ibn al-Hasan ibn 'Ubayd Allah al-Bazzaz recited to me one of their poems:

125

When I wrote to you and you didn't answer
or look to me with a friendly eye,
I made up my mind to get on my horse
and be my own messenger, dropping on by!

161

Al-Husayn ibn 'Ubayd Allah al-Bazzaz recited to me
a poem by one of them:

I invited myself when you didn't invite me,
so the thanks goes to me and not you for my
    luck.
It's better than if you had tried to invite me,
and I'd hurt your feelings by not showing up!

162

Bunan recited to us:

You ask me in when there's nothing to eat,
you shut me out when you're having a feast!
I'd die for you! Could you be any brasher?
Am I not still your party-crasher?

163

Bunan also recited to us:

We slip right through when the crowd's
    a-dashing;
and thus do honor to party-crashing.

Accounts of Bunan,
the Party-Crasher

164

Al-Khatib said:

> Bunan is the most talked-about party-crasher,
> the party-crasher of the farthest-reaching fame.
> And in terms of party-crashing—in terms of the
> extreme lengths to which he goes, as well as his
> customary goings-on—Bunan's got what no one
> else has. News of him abounds; we cited some of
> it already. And now, God willing, we are going to
> present the rest.

165

There is dispute about his name, for he is called
'Abd Allah ibn 'Uthman, and he is also called 'Ali

Bunan

ibn Muhammad. His last name is Bunan, and his agnomen is Abu al-Hasan. He was originally from Merv but resided in Baghdad, and his anecdotes are transmitted on the authority of a number of scholarly people.

129

166

Ahmad ibn Abi Ja'far told me that 'Ali ibn al-Hasan al-Tarsusi in Egypt said, I heard 'Abd Allah ibn 'Adi say, I heard al-Hasan ibn 'Ali Salih saying:

I heard Bunan saying, "I memorized the entire Qur'an, but I've forgotten all but four words: 'Give us our lunch.'"[1]

167

Abu Mansur Muhammad ibn 'Isa al-Hamadhani and Abu al-Qasim 'Ubayd Allah ibn 'Abd al-'Aziz al-Bardha'i and 'Ali ibn Abi 'Ali al-Basri told us, Muhammad ibn 'Ubayd Allah ibn Shukhayr al-Sayrafi related to us, Ahmad ibn al-Hasan ibn 'Ali al-Muqri' related to us:

I heard my father ask Bunan, "Have you memorized a single thing from the Book of God?"
"Yes," Bunan said. "A verse."
"Which one?" he asked.
So Bunan said, "He told his slave, 'Give us our lunch!'"

1. Qur'an 18:62.

Then my father asked, "Have you memorized any poetry?"

Bunan said, "Yes. A line."

He asked, "Which one?

And Bunan recited,

We visit you, forgiving your cruel distance,
for the true lover comes uncalled for.

168

Al-Husayn ibn Muhammad al-Rafiqi informed us, 'Ali ibn al-Sari told us, Ahmad ibn al-Hasan al-Muqri' related to us, Bunan told us, 'Abbas al-Dawri related to me, Abu al-Hasan al-Mada'ini and others of his friends related to me on the authority of 'Ali ibn Suhaym on the authority of al-Sha'bi who said:

They were discussing wedding food around 'Umar ibn al-Khattab, and someone asked him, "O Commander of the Faithful! Why is there a flavor in wedding food that you can't find anywhere else?"

"The Prophet prayed a blessing upon it," he said, "and Abraham also prayed that God bless it and make it tastier, so there's a pinch of the food of Paradise mixed in . . ."

170

Al-Husayn ibn Muhammad al-Rafiqi informed us, 'Ali ibn Muhammad ibn al-Sari told us, Ahmad ibn al-Husayn al-Muqri' told us, I heard Bunan say, Muhammad ibn al-Hasan al-Bazzaz told us, Ibn 'Ali ibn al-Hasan ibn Shaqiq related to me on the authority of his father, Ibn al-Mubarak told me on the authority of al-Mubarak and Rabi', on the authority of al-Hasan who said:

> There are twelve features of mealtime that a Muslim ought to learn: four of them are an obligation from God, four were the customs of the Prophet, and four are a matter of good manners. The four obligatory points are to invoke God before eating, to know which food is forbidden, to take pleasure in it, and to thank God for it. The four customs of the Prophet are to sit on one's left foot while eating, not to reach across the table, to eat with three fingers, and to lick the fingers when finished. As for the matters of good form: one should wash one's hands, take little bites, chew thoroughly, and not stare at friends.

171

'Ubayd Allah ibn 'Abd al-'Aziz al-Bardha'i told us, Ahmad ibn Ibrahim ibn Shadhan told us, Abu Bakr

Ahmad ibn Marwan ibn Muhammad al-Maliki al-Qadi al-Dinawari told us, Muhammad ibn 'Abd al-'Aziz told us, Muhammad ibn Dinar told us, I heard Waki' ibn al-Jarrah say:

> I was eating at the same table as Bunan the party-crasher, and I heard him say to me, "Dammit, Waki'! You're a scholar of the hadith and a jurist of Iraq, and you're eating eggplants—you can buy a hundred eggplants for a small coin, and you're ignoring the chicken breasts, chickens costing a whole dinar?! How little you know!"

172

Al-Bardha'i told us, Ibn Shadhan told us, Ahmad ibn Marwan al-Maliki told us, Muhammad ibn 'Abd al-'Aziz told us, Muhammad ibn Dinar told us, and he said:

> I heard Waki' ibn al-Jarrah say, "Bunan the party-crasher said to me, 'Waki'! Having command of the table is better than having four dishes to yourself!'"

173

Al-Khatib said:

133

There is something very suspicious about this story because Bunan lived after Waki' ibn Jarrah by a long time and a great while; Waki' died in 196, whereas Bunan lived around 300.[2]

174

Another version is also preserved on the authority of Bunan on the authority of Sa'id al-Samin on the authority of Waki':

Abu Talib Yahya ibn 'Ali ibn al-Tayyib al-Daskari told me word for word in Helwan, Abu Bakr ibn al-Muqri' informed us in Isfahan, 'Ali ibn Ishaq al-Madhara'i told us, Bunan the party-crasher told us, Sa'id al-Samin told us, I heard Waki' say, "Having command of the table is better than three dishes!"

175

Abu al-Qasim al-Azhari told me, Muhammad ibn Humayd ibn al-Husayn ibn Humayd ibn al-Rabi' al-Harraz told us, Muhammad ibn al-Hakimi told

---

2. These *hijri* dates are equivalent to about 811 and 912 CE.

us, 'Abd Allah ibn 'Uthman Bunan told us, Sa'id al-Samin informed me on the authority of Waki' al-Jarrah:

> Having command of the table is better than three dishes, and white semolina tastes better than yellow semolina.

176

Abu Mansur Muhammad ibn 'Isa told us, 'Ubayd Allah ibn 'Abd al-'Aziz and 'Ali ibn Abi al-Shakhir informed us, Ahmad ibn al-Hasan ibn 'Ali al-Muqri' informed us:

> I heard Bunan say, "'Abbas al-Dawri informed me, I heard Yahya ibn Ma'in say, 'Eating with friends doesn't hurt!'"

177

Al-Husayn ibn Muhammad al-Rafiqi informed us, 'Ali ibn Muhammad al-Sari told us, Ahmad ibn al-Hasan al-Muqri' told us, Bunan, meaning 'Ali ibn Muhammad 'Uthman, the party-crasher, related to me, Ja'far al-Tayalisi related to me, and he said, I heard Yahya ibn Ma'in say:

When you go to your friend's house, sit down where you are seated and drink what you are given, and do not be a burden on them. If you eat and then wander around and do not sit, you will be a burden on them in their gathering.

178

Ja'far al-Tayalisi said, I heard Bunan say, 'Abbas al-Dawri and al-Saghani said, Yahya ibn Ma'in said:

It is silly to eat abstemiously at the house of one's companions, nor do I condone the practice. Fasting in the house of one's friends is annoying and hypocritical.

179

Abu al-Hasan 'Ali ibn Ayyub al-Qummi told me, Muhammad ibn 'Umran ibn Musa al-Katib told us, al-Suli told me, Abu Hamid ibn al-'Abbas told us:

Bunan, the party-crasher, told me, "I went to Basra and someone told me, 'There's a party-crashing expert here who watches out for party-crashers, clothes them, leads them to gigs, and shares with them.' So I went to him, and he was charitable with me and he clothed me, and I stayed with him for three days. He had shares coming to him from all the party-crashers: they would carry food out of the party and give half to him and keep half for themselves.

So on the fourth day I set out and went to a banquet, and I ate and carried a lot out with me, half of which I gave to him and half of which I kept. I sold my half for some money. I didn't do anything wrong that time.

But one day I went to a glorious wedding, and I ate and carried a nice portion out, and then I met some people who bought it all for a dinar. I took the money and hid it.

The master called a party-crasher meeting, and he said, "This Baghdadi has betrayed us! He thought that I didn't know everything that he does. Smack him and find out what he has hidden from us."

So they made me sit down whether I would or not, and they went on smacking me one by one, and the first one said, "He ate lamb." Then another smacked me and sniffed my hand and said, "He ate vegetables," and another said, "He ate semolina," until they had mentioned each thing that I ate. They didn't miss one thing nor name one extra dish.

Then one gentleman smacked me a great smack and said, "He sold the rest for a dinar," and another smacked me and said, "Give up the dinar," and I handed it over to the chief. He took the robe that he had given me and said, "Leave us, O traitor, without the protection of God."

So I left on a ship and came back to Baghdad, and I vowed not to stay in the land where the party-crashers know the Unknown.[3]

180

Al-Husayn ibn Muhammad al-Rafiqi informed us, 'Ali ibn Muhammad ibn al-Sari told us, Ahmad ibn al-Hasan al-Muqri' told us, I heard Bunan say:

Do not take a weaver or a cupper or a tailor or a donkey driver or an auctioneer as a dinner

---

3. Sufis and mystics were often mockingly likened to party-crashers and accused of posing as poor holy men to obtain free food. In an article van Gelder translates the following eleventh-century quote criticizing Sufis, which might remind readers of the party-crashers (see anecdotes 111, 166, and 197, for example): "Because eating much is their religion . . . they specialise in taking large mouthfuls, in a good digestion, and being opportunistic eaters. . . . They are so much concerned with eating and spending most of their time eating, that one of them inscribed his signet-ring with 'Food Perpetual' [Qur'an 18:62], another inscribed 'Bring Us Our Breakfast' [Qur'an 18:62]" ("Edible Fathers and Mothers," 109).

companion. For a weaver makes cuts all day, and thus his speech is always: "I made a robe with two side cuts today, and then I made three side cuts, and then four, and then five, until there were ten cuts! And tomorrow, God willing, I'll cut a robe for a third and a dirham of a third, and two dirhams of a third, then three for a half and two dirhams with a half and three dirhams! The robe is not wide but is light, and I didn't pound it or scrape it, so it remained coarse . . ." His whole day is robes, "I cut them and I sold them," so you won't get anything good out of a man of this trade.

As for the cupper, from the moment he sits down until the moment he stands up, he is gossiping about people: "I cupped So-and-So and he gave me a dirham, and then I cupped So-and-So and *he* gave me half a dirham! I removed So-and-So's hair and he gave me half a dirham, and then I shaved So-and-So and *he* gave me a dirham! So-and-So is lavish, and So-and-So is stingy . . ." So he talks about every little detail, the motherfucker, from the time he sits down until he stands up again.

And the donkey driver, from the time he sits until he stands: "I lent out a donkey for a *daniq*, and then for two *daniqs*, and then for half a dirham, and we kept lending donkeys until we got a dirham or more. A donkey needs half a dirham to a dirham in grain and a load of dry fodder . . . ," and he will pass an entire day with these petty details.

The tailor, from the time he sits down until the time he stands, talks behind people's backs, saying nasty things about them: "So-and-So is in love with So-and-So, and So-and-So loves somebody else. I made a robe for So-and-So, the songstress, whom So-and-So is falling for, a robe of wrapped linen; he sent her a 'high robe of Merv!'" and he goes on gossiping about people from the time he sits down until the time he stands, the motherfucker.

And the auctioneer: "I sold So-and-So a horse for such-and-such an amount, and I sold a concubine to So-and-So for such-and-such amount, and So-and-So is content, and So-and-So is content . . ." So from the time he sits until he stands, he is gossiping about good Muslims: "And the market inspector apprehended So-and-So and Ms. So-and-So." The party is constantly interrupted by this kind of comment.

O my brother! May I be your ransom! Do not befriend any of this low breed, for they will carry away your good reputation among your friends and your loyal acquaintances. Befriend (may I be your ransom!) cloth merchants, perfumers, money changers, fine carpet salesmen, cotton merchants, millers, and apothecaries. These sorts are like scholars born of scholars, or leaders born of leaders. That is my advice to you.

181

Al-Husayn ibn Muhammad al-Rafiqi informed us, 'Ali ibn Muhammad ibn al-Sari told us, Ahmad ibn al-Hasan al-Muqri' told us:

> Bunan adopted an apprentice and told him, "If you are invited to a banquet (God willing!), beware, oh, beware of delaying until the last hour, or becoming distracted and dragging your feet and saying, "I'll go in an hour," or "No more than an hour," or "What have I forgotten?" or "What if nobody has come and I'm the first one there? Why should I be the first one?" This kind of thing destroys your chances, limits your choices, and leads you to lose the day. These are the actions of ignorant people who do not plan carefully. So if your friend invites you to a party, seek the Lord's guidance and be one of the first people to show up. Take this advice, and you will be rightly guided, and clearly a man of correct conduct, God willing.
>
> Know that he who does not arrive at the earliest moment is not one of the important people, chief among whom is the secretary, the cloth merchant, the apothecary, the saddle maker, and that sort. Sitting with these people is most profitable, for with them you are sure of your happiness, plus you will hear sound conversation and elegant stories. You will be comfortable

and have a roomy seat with the highest class of man, if you sit with them at the first table. Cling to this class of people, and do not let yourself get separated from their sides, lest you be destroyed. You have nothing to lose, even if you gain nothing.

Sitting at the first table to be brought out has many praiseworthy characteristics. Know, O ignorant, that there you may take the first portion from the pots; there you will find plenty of everything: the pots will be full, the water cold, the bread hot, the master of the feast fresh and happy, and everything at your command. You have plenty of room, and are sitting with a group as good as gold, livelier than the first fruits, aware of what they're eating, with no tasty food or delicious drink unknown to them. Eating with these men is easy and safe, and everything that you eat and drink will be wholesome to you.

If you make a speedy departure for the party, it will come as a relief to your host. He will know that he has done his duty by you, and his heart will be untroubled. But if you delay and laze about until the last minute, then all is lost and destroyed by your languishment. Know that you will find only cold food and leftovers, and picked-over loaves (the good ones having been taken), and warm water, and a peevish, exasperated host who wishes, at the moment, that you'd go to hell. Also know, my brother, that at the last table brought out, the pickings are scarce, because ten people were planned for and thirty were served, so each man can have only a bite or two of every dish, which a number of hands will have pawed over, and your seat will be too small for your body. The moment the host calls to those last people to eat, they will rush to the table, scattering all over and ripping off the veil of good manners, standing shoulder to shoulder like buildings built side by side, eating from the right, the left, and the middle, their hands ranging around the table from east to west, and you'll hear the gurgling in their throats. That is because the only people who sit at the last table are the poor and the weak, and a lamb or a kid doesn't mean a thing to them but a chance to gorge themselves. Were they presented with a prime rib of lamb, served with the skin still on and lettuce and endives on the side, soon it would be like a hut whose walls had fallen with only the beams still standing. So what will be the state of one who sits with this lowest breed of manhood? He won't eat a little and he won't eat a lot, but he'll get up from the table with a heart more desolate than the heart of Moses's mother, hungry and thirsty, having had no more of the banquet than the smell of the food and the marrow of the bones.

I have explained this to you so that you may understand that I have advised you to the limits of advising, and taught you as Sufyan al-Thawri taught in his school,[4] and caused you to learn manners and culture. May God bless you with a patient heart, delicious food, and a sturdy jaw . . . though such a prayer is not likely to be heeded.

182

Bunan said:

If your friend invites you to a meal, sit on the right side of the house, because from there you can see everything that you want, and hold sway over them all. You will be the first to get everything, the first to wash his hands, with the table all in front of you. You will drink from the first bottle, the good vegetables will be placed in front of you, you will be the first to be perfumed, for if you are sitting at the edge of the table, you have nothing to do but keep track of what is coming and going, and you are steeped in every pleasure until you depart.

4. Sufyan al-Thawri was a famous Islamic scholar from the eighth century.

183

Al-Husayn ibn Muhammad al-Rafiqi informed us, 'Ali ibn Muhammad ibn al-Sari told us, Ahmad ibn al-Hasan al-Muqri' told us, and he said:

> I heard Bunan say, "The tastiest thing that could be are eggplants in *sikbaj*, and *al-hisrimiyya*, and *al-madira*, and *al-kashkiyya*," and "The tastiest thing that could be is the meat of a lamb in *'adasiyya*, and *al-madira*, and *al-hisrimiyya*, and *al-kashkiyya*."[5]

184

Bunan said, "The tail of a goat is better than a whole pot of beans."

185

He said:

5. Recipes for *sikbaj*, *hisrimiyya*, and *madira* can be found in the chapter on sour dishes in Charles Perry's *Baghdad Cookery Book*, a translation of a thirteenth-century Arabic cookbook. A recipe for *'adasiyya* can be found in the chapter on plain dishes.

I heard Bunan say, "Food taken with friends is easily digested. Food taken with boors is ill-digested."

186

Al-Rafiqi informed us, Ibn al-Sari told us, Ahmad ibn al-Hasan al-Muqri' told us, I heard Ja'far ibn Yahya al-Mada'ini say, a friend of mine related to me:

I was sitting with Bunan at a table, and he said to me, "Do not contradict anything that I'm about to say to you."

They brought out a large wooden bowl of semolina, and he said to me, "Eat only the red part, because there are two flavors in it: the flavor of sugar and the flavor of saffron." He did not invite me to eat any other part. "Hold yourself back," he said.

Then they brought *harisa*, and he said to me, "Eat one, two, or three bites."[6]

Then they brought red *zirbaj* soup, and he said to me, "Eat a bite or two."

Then they brought us dried fried meat, and he said to me, "Don't eat but a bite or two, and

---

6. *Harisa* is made of meat and wheat pounded together. Charles Perry's *Baghdad Cookery Book* includes several recipes.

no more, and throw the dry bread to the dogs"
(meaning that in which the meat was wrapped).

Then they brought us vegetables, and he said
to me, "Eat a bite or two."

Then they brought us some roast meat, and
he said to me, "Don't eat any of it. Hold yourself
back. Every day we can buy some roast meat for
only a *daniq* that would replace what is here quite
well."

Then they brought us some *faludhaj*, and
there was a great deal of it heaped up in a cone
shape, and he said to me, "Take from the bottom
until it collapses."

So I did, and he said to me, "Eat and take
more. This you don't see every day."

How Many

Then they brought us some *lawzinaj*. "Double or triple your portion," he said, "and if it kills you, you'll die a martyr."

Then they brought us a plate of a fattened, roasted chicken, and he ate two or three times his portion, and he said to me, "Eat and don't cut it short, because this is valued at three dinars. Eat only things that have value." So he ate two of them, and I ate three.

(Those may not be his exact words.)[7]

188

Al-Rafiqi informed us, Ibn al-Sari told us, Ahmad ibn al-Hasan told us:

Someone asked Bunan, "What do you think about *faludhaj*?"

"By God!" he answered. "It is of the food of Paradise! Should anyone asking about *faludhaj* in this earthly life refer to intellect or reason? You simpleton! Eat it—forever until you die! And

---

7. Anecdote 187, missing because it defied my powers of translation, can be found translated by Fedwa Malti-Douglas in her article "Structure and Organization in a Monographic *Adab* Work: *Al-tatfil* of al-Khatib al-Baghdadi," 235-36. It has to do with Bunan's citation of a property law in defense of his stealing meat from a fellow diner.

when you die, die full-bellied, and may you find your reward with the Almighty God."

190

Al-Husayn ibn Muhammad al-Rafiqi informed us, 'Ali ibn Muhammad al-Sari told us, Ahmad ibn al-Hasan al-Muqri' told us, Wasif al-Banna said:

Bunan came up to me at a wedding, and I said to him, "You're crowding me!"

"If I'm doing you no benefit," he replied, "then let me do you no harm!"

I sneezed.

"Raise your head up," he said, "and breathe deeply three times. It will ease your swallowing."

191

Al-Rafiqi informed us, Ibn al-Sari told us, Ahmad ibn al-Hasan told us:

I hear Bunan say, "Taking from two plates, plus some cold water, is the dearest thing to me."

192

Abu al-Hasan Bunan said:

When, having eaten, you get up from the table, sit in the middle of the house where a cool draft will hit you, and call for some drink. If they bring you date wine, I prefer to take a measure or two, and don't dilute it with water. If they bring beer, don't drink too much, or it will make you queasy. If they toast you, they have invited you into their private dwelling, but do not sit at the seat farthest from the door, because that seat is for singers, or for the decrepit, and if you want to go get something or urinate, it is difficult to get up, and other people at the table will be incommoded by your rising. So sit by the door.

If there is a lot of fruit in the house, pull it over to your side; don't trust that it will come to you and just sit around waiting with nothing. Don't designate yourself the wine pourer; be the tail, not the head.

If there's a songstress or a slave boy with an attractive face at the party, fear God in your heart and do not become enamored with them. Look to your own welfare, for as God Almighty said in His book, "Strain not thine eyes for the splendor we have bestowed on this earthly life . . ."[8]

If the wine is passed around in cups, see that the better part of it stays where you are sitting,

8. Qur'an 20:131.

and take it by the bottle or the cup and drink it yourself.

If you see people confusing their conversation, and there is grape wine at the gathering, fear God and do not drink it, and do not linger where grape wine's to be had, for 'Ali ibn Sahl ibn al-Mughira related to me, as did 'Ali ibn al-Hasan ibn Salih al-Razi, both transmitting on the authority of Mu'awiya, on the authority of the Prophet, who said, "Whosoever drinks grape wine, flog him. If he does it repeatedly, kill him."[9] O my brother! Beware, beware of drunkenness! For if the crowd sees you stumble or bungle your speech, they will judge you by it. Though your reputation with your neighbors may be spotless, when you walk away your reputation will be soiled, and though you may be the leader of the Friday service or give the call to prayer, that kind of humiliation never fades. Rather, you must tell excellent stories or excellent hadith, and everyone will grow to like you, and you will become master

9. The date wine mentioned was probably less fermented than the grape wine. As for the hadith prescribing punishment of chronic drunkenness with death, it was "added in some traditions that capital punishment in such cases is not according to the *sunna* of the Prophet." *The Encyclopaedia of Islam*, s.v. "Khamr." Indeed, it seems that the implementation of such a punishment would have resulted in a veritable massacre.

of them all. But if you become confused, and passionate, and unruly, it is a slap to the face, and it breeds enmity among your neighbors that never fades. So beware, my brother, of drunkenness! Drink five cups, six cups, seven cups, but don't become drunk. If you take care against drunkenness, when you rise up, you are sound and have your intelligence. May God save us, and beware, my brother, of the passing of this earthly life and the coming of the other. Take my advice, and you will be guided aright, God willing.

194

Bunan called white bread "Abu Na'im" (Mr. Fine), course bread "Abu Jabir" (Mr. Force), semolina "Abu Surur" or "Abu Malik" (Mr. Joy and Mr. Royalty), meat "Abu 'Asim" (Mr. Hold Fast), greens "Abu Jamil" (Mr. Beautiful), vinegar "Abu Thaqif" (Mr. Strong [Vinegar]), lamb "Abu Humayd" (Mr. Little Laudable), kid "Abu Habib" (Mr. Darling), chicken "Umm al-Khayr" (Mrs. Good), duck "Umm 'Amr" (Mrs. Life), brain "Abu al-Raja'" (Mr. Anticipation), trotter "Abu al-Ghasha" (Mr. Swoon), cheese "Rashid al-Khaniq" (Rashid the Strangler), olives "Khanafis al-Khiwan" (beetle of the serving tray), salt fish "Umm al-Balaya" (Mrs. Calamity), *mabaqali* "Abu al-Riyah" (Mr. Wind), *faludhaj* "Abu al-'Ala" (Mr. Exalted), pudding "Abu Razin" (Mr. Heavy), *lawzinaj* "Qubur al-Atfal" (Children's Tombs), honey doughnuts "Qubur al-Shuhada'" (Martyr's Tombs), *'asida* pastries "Umm Sahl" (Mrs. Smooth), water "Abu al-Ghayth" (Mr. Big Rain), drinking buddies "Abu al-Kamal" (Mr. Perfect), social gatherings "Abu Mahmud" (Mr. Praised), minarets and lamps "Abu Siyah" (Mr. Clamor), toothpicks "Kitab al-'Azl" (the Book of Removal), and potash "Abu al-Ya's" (Mr. Despair).[10]

197

Ahmad ibn Muhammad ibn Ahmad al-'Atiqi told us, Sahl ibn Ahmad ibn Sahl al-Dibaji told us, Abu Bakr ibn al-Anbari told us, Ahmad ibn Mansur told us, Ahmad ibn 'Ali said:

A man asked Bunan to pray on his behalf, so he raised his hand and said, "May God graciously bestow bodily health upon you, and a lot of food, and a lengthy appetite, and a strong stomach. May he grant you teeth that grind and a stomach

10. In his article "Edible Fathers and Mothers," van Gelder describes the widespread use of these nicknames for food, particularly among party-crashers, and provides a complete list. *Abu* and *Umm*, here translated as "Mr." and "Mrs.," actually mean "father" and "mother."

that digests, as well as holding capacity, even temperament, security, and vigor." Then he said, "Such a prayer is not likely to be heeded."

198

Al-Rafiqi informed us, Ibn al-Sari told us, Ahmad ibn al-Hasan told us:

I heard Bunan say, "I saw my son smacking his lips one day, so I incanted a prayer, saying, 'May you prove a worthy successor'" (meaning in party-crashing).

199

He said:

I heard Bunan say, "There is nothing in the world better than my profession. I've been a party-crasher thirty years, and I've never taken on a single apprentice."

200

He said:

I heard Bunan say, "Taking charge of a banquet you didn't throw is a shame, but if you did throw it, it's a big shame."

201

He said:

I heard Bunan say, "Petty bickering at a party is one of the worst two disasters that can befall you."

202

He said:

Bunan went to a party and walked inside. "Who are you?" they asked him.

"I am he who spared you the trouble of sending an invitation!" he replied.

203

He said:

Someone said to Bunan, "Which kind of food do you find tastiest?"

"Whatever makes its owner feel most generous!" he replied.

204

He said:

I heard Bunan say, "There are several things that drain, nay, kill, a banquet: if the host is stingy, and the gatekeeper is a pompous liar, the steward is a lowlife of little learning, the cook isn't good at his job and has dirty hands, and the table and the sitting place for the partygoers is as bare of singers and wine as a ruin is.

"Seven things by which the pleasure and happiness of the guests can be increased are: if the host of the banquet is generous and magnanimous and openhanded, and never asked for anything he doesn't give. If the doorman is witty and understanding, and the house manager, or steward, is intelligent and cultured, and guides the people to their seats and arranges them, and the cook is good at his job and has clean hands, and the serving boy is intelligent and laughs with the guests, encouraging them to eat, and when the people whom you love and who love you are seated at the table, eating together with you, and nobody troublesome or repulsive comes and jostles or annoys you, but your intelligent friends who understand you come, and are generous with you and honor you and insist that you eat more, and their joy appears in their faces. I pray to God for these men and their offspring.

"It does not behoove you to despise anyone except the stingy, the low, or those with a flaw in their genealogy, but a gathering with good singers and wine is like someone relating a story to an eager audience."

205

He said:

> I heard Bunan say, "If you are invited to two par-
> ties, go to the one closer to you."

206

Al-Khatib said, there is a tradition of the Prophet
similar to this, which was told to us by al-Hasan ibn
'Ali al-Tamimi, that Ahmad ibn Ja'far ibn Hamdan
told us, 'Abd Allah ibn Ahmad ibn Hanbal told us,
my father related to me, 'Abd al-Salam ibn Harb told
us, Yazid ibn 'Abd al-Rahman al-Dalani told me, on
the authority of Abu al-'Ala' al-Awdi, on the authority of Humayd ibn 'Abd al-Rahman, on the authority of one of the companions of the Prophet, peace
and prayers upon him, who said:

> If two people invite you, answer the one who is
> closest to you, for that one is your closest neigh-
> bor. If one of them asks you before the other,
> answer the one that asked first.

207

Abu Nu'aym al-Hafiz told us, 'Abd Allah ibn Ja'far
ibn Ahmad ibn Faris told us, Yunus ibn Habib told us,

Abu Dawud told us, Shu'ba told us on the authority of Abu 'Imran on the authority of Talha ibn 'Ubayd Allah, on the authority of 'A'isha, who said:

> "Prophet of God, I have two neighbors. Which of them should I head for more?"
>
> "Whoever's door is closer to you," he said.

208

Muhammad ibn 'Ali al-Jallab told me:

> Bunan heard a man say, "The Antichrist will emerge in a year of drought, bringing cakes of bread from Isfahan, rock salt, and *asafetida* of Sarkhas."
>
> "God help you!" he said. "This is a man who deserves to be heard and obeyed!"

209

Al-Rafiqi informed us, Ibn al-Sari told us, Ahmad ibn al-Hasan al-Muqri' told us:

> I heard Bunan the party-crasher say, "A friend of mine invited me to a party he was having for merchants. I asked him for some sweet butter paste, so he brought me some fruit butter, fresh and

untouched by fire, along with flower sifted with two sieves, fine and coarse. It looked like gold filings in a crucible, with Arabic butter of Basra, in a large, burnished copper pot with a strong forearm. (The sign that the flour is cooked is that it says 'Tuf tuf,' and the sign that the butter is cooked is that it says 'Baq baq')

"Then we were brought a polished wooden skull bowl, and he threw everything in and shook it until it was mixed. Then a large shallow pan was brought out to fry it in, and I spied in the middle a burial of butter.

"A group of jokers were sitting with us who had not yet recognized me, and one of them took a bite, getting part of the butter.

"'They were thrown in headlong, with the straying,' he said, and he pulled the butter closer to himself.[11]

"Another of them said, while all were digging in, 'They heard it raging and sighing,' and he pulled the butter over to himself.[12] The butter was dwindling.

11. All of these quotes are passages from the Qur'an, taken amusingly out of context. This quote is from 26:94 and refers to hellfire (though in this context, it refers to the pan).

12. "They heard it raging" is from Qur'an 25:12 and also refers to hellfire (used here for the sounds of the cooking butter).

"'The ruined well and the lofty tower,' I remarked, and tore the butter away.[13]

"Then another one said, 'Did you tear it to drown its people? Truly you have done a shocking thing,' and he pulled the butter over.[14]

"'We lead the water to a parched land,' I replied, and tore the butter away.[15]

"'Two springs are gushing within,' said another, and pulled the butter toward himself.[16]

"'Two springs are flowing within,' I replied, and tore the butter away.[17]

"'We caused the water to gather as ordained,' said another, and pulled the butter toward himself.[18]

13. "The ruined well" is from Qur'an 22:45 and refers to the disobedient civilizations destroyed by God (used here for the dwindling butter supply).

14. "Did you tear it" is from Qur'an 18:71 and refers to a ship (here used for the butter bowl, and the butter from now on is likened to water).

15. "We lead the water" is from Qur'an 32:27 and refers to God causing rain.

16. "Two springs are gushing" is from Qur'an 55:66 and refers to Paradise.

17. "Two springs are flowing" is from Qur'an 55:50, earlier in the same description.

18. "We caused the water" is from Qur'an 54:12.

"'And then led it to a dead land,' I replied, and tore the butter away.[19]

"I saw that no one was going to speak, and so I went on, 'It was said, "O Earth, swallow the waters," and "Clear, O Sky," and the waters subsided, the commandment was fulfilled, and it came to rest on the mountain, and it was said, "Begone, ye unrighteous!"' and I mixed the butter with what was left of the fruit paste.[20]

"They laughed, and one of them began to choke, so everyone had to pound him on the back until the morsel went down. Thank God he was not harmed!"

210

Al-Rafiqi informed us, Ibn al-Sari told us, Ahmad ibn al-Hasan al-Muqri' told us, saying, I heard Abu ʿAbd Allah Husayn ibn Jaʿfar al-Kufi say to Bunan:

Bunan the party-crasher related to me, "Muhammad ibn ʿAbd Allah ibn Tahir held a banquet. I

19. "And then led it" is from Qur'an 35:9 and also refers to water.

20. "It was said, 'O Earth'" is from Qur'an 11:44 and refers to Noah's ark (used here for Bunan's triumphant conclusion of the butter contest).

went," he said, "and entered with those going in. We were heading for the best table, where the Banu Hashim were, and Muhammad ibn 'Abd Allah called Bishr ibn Harun, his secretary.

"'Damn it!' he said. 'Who's the guy with the round cap . . . I mean the one with a tall black hat on his head and a green mantle—the one I don't know?'

"'My lord,' he said, 'that man is called Bunan. He attends these banquets whether he is invited or not.'

"'O Bishr!' said Muhammad ibn 'Abd Allah ibn Tahir. 'If he has eaten, bring him to me!'

"When Bunan was fetched, Muhammad asked him, 'Who you?' (meaning 'Who are you?').

"'May God extend the life of the prince!' he replied. 'I'm the man who is attending these banquets whether I am invited or not.'

"'Deliver your requests to me,' he answered.

"'My lord,' said Bunan, 'I request that you write a certificate for me saying that no one may join in this craft (or perhaps he said "profession") unless he is freed to do so by my hand.'

"He wrote the document as described and ordered one hundred dinars be given to Bunan.

"Abu 'Abd Allah Ahmad ibn al-Hasan said, 'I read the document, which was in the calligraphy of Bishr al-Nasrani.'"

A Document Pertaining
to Party-Crashing

The judge Abu al-Qasim 'Ali ibn al-Muhassin ibn 'Ali al-Tanukhi related to me:

> Among the retinue of the Amir Bakhtiyar,[1] known as 'Izz al-Dawla, was a man named 'Aliyyaka,

1. In the year 967, 'Izz al-Dawla reigned in Baghdad. An ineffectual ruler, absorbed by petty pleasures and prone to meddle frivolously in government affairs, 'Izz was nonetheless responsible for the following invaluable document, which, in the course of appointing Baghdad's first official officer of party-crashing, offered instruction in this obscure, but profitable, refinement. Written by Secretary Abu Ishaq Ibrahim ibn Hilal al-Sabi in the voice of 'Aliyyaka, a party-crasher, the document appointed Ibn 'Urs al-Mawsili officer of party-crashing.

who was a great party-crasher of military men (the gatekeepers, officers, and secretaries), and of the prominent members of the private class, as well as male concubines. Bakhtiyar got wind of this and ordained that 'Aliyyaka should appoint a successor in party-crashing. He approached the scribe Abu Ishaq Ibrahim ibn Hilal al-Sabi with the task of writing this appointment for Ibn 'Urs al-Mawsili on the authority of 'Aliyyaka, making Ibn 'Urs his successor in party-crashing. Abu Ishaq wrote the document for him in a humorous fashion and read it to us. This was the text:

> These are the tasks with which 'Ali ibn Ahmad, known as 'Aliyakka, entrusted 'Ali ibn 'Urs al-Mawsili when he deputized him, that he may thereby propagate his doctrine. 'Aliyakka appointed al-Mawsili in order to preserve the practice of his art for the people of the city of Baghdad, the City of Peace, as well as to record what is to be obtained under party-crashing's auspices, both its core practices as well as its fringe elements.
>
> Al-Mawsili is appointed in recognition of his lack of shame, his aggressive social intercourse, his frequency of mouthfuls taken, and his stellar digestive ability. He is noted for his energetic pursuit of this little-known practice in

which he excels, and this undercultivated art that he knows so well, for by its means he obtains the blessings of voluptuous food and physical pleasure. He is a frequent visitor of the well-to-do with variegated resources; God gave him power over rarities of foodstuffs, and gave him victory over marvelous delicacies, and he therefore takes a share of the goods as though he were a major investor in their business. He charms his way through the door, making a surprising entrance, using methods that shall be laid bare by this document, as the righteous and proper mode of conduct shall be exhaustively detailed. May God grant me success, for to Him turn petitioners, and in Him we trust.

I command the party-crasher to fear God, the most powerful, the fortified fortress, the unshakable pillar, the lofty mountain, the reinforced defense, the walled garden, and the blessed provision for the day of Resurrection, on which day none but a party-crasher shall obtain provision! I order him to declare his piety privately and openly, to be observant in his words and in his deeds, to make God's pleasure his goal, His reward his desire, nearness to Him

165

his wish, and praising Him his purpose. Nor shall he with overhasty step stray from his Lord, lest he be faced with punishment and repining.

I command him to contemplate party-crashing and its meaning, its purport and its methods, and to conduct his own scholarly investigation with original research, rather than mere imitation or citation. Many people find the practice truly despicable, and loathe the people who do it, accusing them of being mischievous and greedy, but some of these men are faulty in their reasoning and infelicitous in their speech. Some of them are also stingy with their money and hoard it with trickery. Both types are blameworthy, and neither denuded of the trappings of shame.

There is another class of men who do not believe in private property; they spend their own wealth, and drain the wealth of others in the process. They think the best way to enjoy a dinner party is to attack the food, or at a drinking party to guzzle and steal drinks. They are most deserving of the name "noble," best suited for laudation, most appropriately deemed man's men, and the first to be called young knights. Their practice is known as party-crashing, and for men of intelligence there is no shame in it at all. The word is derived from the root *tafala*, which means evening and dusk, but parties can be crashed in both the front and the back part of the day, its beginning and its end, just as the sun and the moon are called "the two moons," but one of them is *the* moon, and just as Abu Bakr and 'Umar are called "the two 'Umars," but one of them is *the* 'Umar.

I command him to attend to the banquets of the noble and the notable at their hosted affairs, and the table spreads of commanders and viziers at their palaces, and thereby to avail himself of easy booty, and gain access to rare delicacies. By seeking out these men, he may hit upon some exquisite foods, the delights of the palate, marvelous eatables, tasty to the gullet. One finds that sort of thing with those sorts of people, and nowhere else.

I command him to attach himself to a rich trader, or to a wealthy city merchant throwing a housewarming feast or an inn-warming feast. These people heap favors on themselves for special occasions, though they are tightfisted in their regular affairs.

167

I command him to befriend the house stewards and their overseers, and keep company with the kitchen managers and their porters. They hold their employers' feasts and drinking parties by the reins and can turn them to the advantage of cohorts and acquaintances. The party-crasher is fortunate in their company, he benefits from their friendship, and his desires are fulfilled in their vicinity.

I command him to attend the merchants' markets and the vendors' fairs. If he sees a large food purchase being made, and somebody jostling to buy provisions, let him follow the purchases to their intended destination and to the house that will receive them. Let him discover the time set for the feast and the gentlemen of leisure who will attend. Without fail, one of these gentlemen will know him, so he can learn the time of his departure and follow him out, waylay him, accompany him, and ultimately go in with him. Barring that, he may commingle with a group of people entering the party. All he has to do is pass through the door and circumvent the authority of the guard and the gatekeeper. Thus, he gains access to what few have gained access to and declined, unless they were already stuffed with food and bleeding wine.

I command him to install spies where singers and entertainers, dykes and cross-dressers live. When these people get news of a party, they go together, or if they get news of a banquet, they all gather there. He must spur his camel on and wear his mount thin getting to this party. He must attack like a devouring whale, a swallowing serpent, a ravaging lion, or the eagle when it strikes.

I command him to avoid poor commoners' parties, troops of the no-good ragtag, not to take one step in their direction, nor part his lips for their food, nor bring his bag of tricks to their doorstep, nor count a man among them a gentleman. Their band combines narrow-mindedness with narrow means, piddling property with paltry power. It is a disgraceful injustice to sponge off of these people, and an insult to the honor of the party-crasher. So avoiding it is best and refraining from it most advisable.

I command him to render an accurate account of what is laid out on the table, and of the food that is there transmitted, until, by means of estimation and approximation, exploration and investigation, he knows the number of dishes, many or few, and their varieties, toothsome and delicious. He thereby enables himself to fill his stomach with the last of them and feel sated just as the meal ends. Whether there is a little or a lot, let his portion never escape him. Let him miss nothing, whether trivial or sublime. When he perceives that the food is scanty and insufficient for the crowd, let him devote himself with shrewd attention and discernment in the matter, and fill his stomach with both hot and cold. He who does so will be safe from the consequences that fall upon amateurs. Those who play coy and politely eat lightly think that the repast will last them until the end of their hunger and finish them in the outer limits of satiety. But it is not long before they are smitten with the discombobulation of a lover and find themselves aching with disappointment. May God preserve us from such a state and guard us from this distressing fate!

I command him to train himself, to redirect his emotions, and ignore what would annoy him; let it pass. Let him feel it best to turn a deaf ear to an obscene insult and to disregard a rude remark. If someone jostles him away, let him patiently wait to receive what is his right. If a smack falls on his head, let him pretend not to notice, so as not to lose his molar's favorite grazing ground. If he meets a snob, let him face him with kindness and serenity. If he penetrates the gates, mingles with the crowd, sits with those present, and blends with the congregation, he will inevitably encounter some disapproving soul, someone who notes that his face is unfamiliar. If this person is modest and high-class, he will hold his tongue, deeming speaking out beneath him. But if this person is a rude, boorish man, he will clear his throat and begin to tell all. Should this happen, the party-crasher must avoid being rude and use kindness with the speaker, thereby curbing his wrath, dulling his sword, and allaying his anger. But if, as time goes on, the others have looked on him again and again, and have grown accustomed to his face, and he comes to seem familiar to them, and they come to like him, then he achieves the same status as the others gathered there, who went through much more trouble to achieve it. We have heard that a man of this sort, a man of understanding and knowledge, intellect and discrimination, crashed a banquet of a very important person. The eyes of the crowd penetrated him, and suspicions ranged freely among them.

"Who are you, may God give you strength?" one asked him.

"I was the first one invited to this event," he said.

"How can that be when we don't even know you?" someone asked.

"If I see the owner of this house, he'll recognize me, and then I'll introduce myself!"

They brought the owner of the house, and when the party-crasher saw him, he greeted him first, saying, "Didn't you tell your cook, may God give you support, to make more than enough food for the number of expected guests and more than the amount that they need to eat?"

"Yes!" he said.

"That excess is for me and those like me. By its means you support those of my calling. It is our daily bread granted by God through your hands. He works through you."

"Welcome!" said the owner of the house. "Make yourself at home. May you sit only with the highest-class people, among table companions and gentlemen. You spoke artfully and well. Let this man be a leader for us to follow and a guide who instructs us by example, God willing!"

I command him to take many digestive aids, which relieve blockages, strengthen the stomach, render food more appetizing, and help process a meal. It bolsters his stamina, thereby improving the regulation of his humors. It calls him to nature twice; twice a day he will rise up after eating. The party-crasher who takes digestive aids is like the writer who sharpens his pens, the soldier who polishes his sword, the craftsman who whets his instruments, or the expert who hones his tools.

This document was charged by 'Ali ibn Ahmad, known as 'Aliyakka, and he will hold you to the injunctions here laid out. He spared you herein no manner of guidance or success, refinement or cultivation, description or observation, incitement or reminder. Be by its decree counseled, by its restrictions curbed, by its illustrations guided, and by its memorization informed, if God so wills. Peace upon you, and the mercy and blessings of the Almighty.

173

Bibliography

Editions and Translations of al-Khatib al-Baghdadi's *Kitab al-tatfil*

L'arte dello scrocco. Translated by Antonella Ghersetti. Cantazaro: Abramo, 2006.

Al-tatfil wa hikayat al-tufayliyin wa akhbaruhum wa nawadir kalamihim wa ash'aruhum. Edited by Bassam 'Abd al-Wahhab al-Jabi. 1999. Reprint, Beirut: Dar Ibn Hazm, 2006.

Al-tatfil wa hikayat al-tufayliyin wa akhbaruhum wa nawadir kalamihim wa ash'aruhum. Edited by 'Abd Allāh 'Abd al-Raḥīm 'Usaylan. Jedda: Dar al-Madani, 1406/1986.

Al-tatfil wa hikayat al-tufayliyin wa akhbaruhum wa nawadir kalamihim wa ash'aruhum. Cairo: Maktaba al-Qudsi, 1983.

Al-tatfil wa hikayat al-tufayliyin wa akhbaruhum wa nawadir kalamihim wa ash'aruhum. Edited by Kazim al-Muzaffar. Najaf: Maktaba al-Haydariya, 1966.

Bibliography

Al-tatfil wa hikayat al-tufayliyin wa akhbaruhum wa nawadir kalamihim wa ash'aruhum. Edited by Husam al-Din Qudsi. Damascus: al-Qudsi, 1927.

Secondary Sources

Bauer, Thomas. "In Search of 'Post-classical Literature': A Review Article." *Mamluk Studies Review* 11, no. 2 (2007).

al-Hibri, Tayeb. *Reinterpreting Islamic Historiography.* Cambridge: Cambridge University Press, 1999.

Malti-Douglas, Fedwa. "Structure and Organization in a Monographic Adab Work: *Al-tatfil* of al-Khatib al-Baghdadi." *Journal of Near Eastern Studies* 40, no. 3 (1981).

Perry, Charles, trans. *A Baghdad Cookery Book.* By Muhammad ibn al-Hasan al-Baghdadi. Devon: Prospect Books, 2005.

Robinson, Chase. *Islamic Historiography.* Cambridge: Cambridge University Press, 2003.

van Gelder, Geert Jan. "Edible Fathers and Mothers." In *El Banquete de las Palabras,* edited by Manuela Marín and Cristina de la Puente. Madrid: Consejo Superior de Investigaciones Científicas, 2005.

———. "Forbidden Firebrands: Frivolous *Iqtibas* (Quotations from the Qur'an) According to Medieval Arab Critics." *Quaderni di Studi Arabi* (Istituto per l'Oriente) 20–21 (2002–3).

———. *Of Dishes and Discourse: Classical Arabic Literary Representations of Food.* Richmond and Surrey: Curzon, 2000.

Emily Selove received her PhD from the University of California in Los Angeles. She was a research associate at the University of Manchester from 2012 to 2014 and is now a lecturer in the Institute of Arab and Islamic Studies at the University of Exeter.